New Proof of God & Satan

James L. Ryave

Published by Bring Humanity Together, LLC

Winter Garden, Florida

TABLE OF CONTENTS

COPYRIGHT PAGE I

DEDICATION III

RELEVANT SCRIPTURES IV

FOREWORD VI

PREFACE TO THE NEW EDITION VII

AUTHOR'S INTRODUCTION 1

CHAPTER 1: THE GOALS FOR THIS BOOK 5

CHAPTER 2: BACKGROUND ON MY SITUATION 9

CHAPTER 3: GOD ENGAGES ME TO DECEIVE SATAN 23

CHAPTER 4: THE PHOTOGRAPH – SATAN'S THREAT IS REVEALED! 27

CHAPTER 5: THE IMPORTANCE OF A LASTING VISUAL PROOF OF SATAN 33

CHAPTER 6: MY PERSONAL TRANSFORMATION 47

CHAPTER 7: DEMONIC INTIMIDATION AFTER THE PHOTOGRAPH 58

CHAPTER 8: THE IMMORTALITY OF THE SOUL 77

CHAPTER 9: HOW DEMONS AFFECT HUMAN BEINGS 89

CHAPTER 10: HOW TO PROTECT YOURSELF AND OTHERS AGAINST EVIL 117

CHAPTER 11: REDUCING THE INCIDENCE OF SUICIDE .. 124

CHAPTER 12: REDUCING SUBSTANCE ABUSE AND BEHAVIORAL ADDICTIONS 127

CHAPTER 13: COUNTERING LONELINESS CAUSED BY DEMONIC ISOLATION 132

CHAPTER 14: ADDRESSING PROBLEMS OF COMMUNICATION AND HATRED............ 138

CHAPTER 15: REDUCING GUN VIOLENCE AND MASS SHOOTINGS 153

CHAPTER 16: A SOLUTION TO PREVENT NUCLEAR WAR...165

CHAPTER 17: SOLVING THE WORLD'S PROBLEMS BY BRINGING HUMANITY TOGETHER............................ 169

CHAPTER 18: IMPLICATIONS FOR PHYSICAL HEALTHCARE... 174

CHAPTER 19: IMPLICATIONS FOR MENTAL HEALTHCARE... 182

CHAPTER 20: IMPROVING LAW ENFORCEMENT & COMMUNITY RELATIONS 187

CHAPTER 21: AUTOBIOGRAPHY AND PERSPECTIVE ON FAITH... 194

CHAPTER 22: HISTORIC IMPORTANCE OF FAITH IN THE UNITED STATES 218

CHAPTER 23: CONCERNS REGARDING THE COVID-19 PANDEMIC.. 218

CHAPTER 24: A CALL TO ACTION 244

CHAPTER 25: CONCLUDING REMARKS 247

ACKNOWLEDGEMENTS.. 255

ABOUT THE AUTHOR 256

APPENDIX A: HELPFUL PRAYERS 257

APPENDIX B: RESOURCES IN THE UNITED STATES FOR THOSE SUFFERING.. 275

PREVENT CHILD ABUSE... 277

PREVENT CRUELTY TO ANIMALS 283

PREVENT DOMESTIC VIOLENCE................................. 288

PREVENT HUMAN TRAFFICKING... 290
PREVENT SUBSTANCE ABUSE... 296
PREVENT SUICIDE... 298
SEEK MENTAL HEALTHCARE 300

COPYRIGHT PAGE

New Proof of God & Satan

Published by Bring Humanity Together, LLC

(https://www.bringhumanitytogether.com/)

Winter Garden, Florida, United States

ISBN: 978-1-953341-19-8

Library of Congress Control Number: 2020917425

Cover art: Archangel Michael by Bill Singleton, whose website is http://billsingleton.net/

Cover Design: James Laurence Ryave

Title Page art: Image by OpenClipart-Vectors from Pixabay (7/22/20)

DEDICATION

Dedicated with infinite love and gratitude to all my loved ones on Earth as well as in Heaven

RELEVANT SCRIPTURES

How you are fallen from heaven, O Day
Star, son of Dawn! ("Lucifer" renamed
"Satan") How you are cut down to the
ground, you who laid the nations low!
You said in your heart, "I will raise my
throne above the stars of God; I will sit
on the mount of assembly on the heights
of Zaphon; I will ascend to the tops of the
clouds, I will make myself like the Most
High." But you are brought down to
Sheol, to the depths of the Pit.

Isaiah 14:12 – 14:15 (NRSV-CE)
+ (Author's note in parentheses)

He (Jesus) said to them, "I watched Satan fall
from heaven like a flash of lightning…."

Luke 10:18 (NRSV-CE)
+ (Author's note in parentheses)

And even if our gospel is veiled, it is veiled to those who are perishing. In their case the god of this world (Satan) has blinded the minds of the unbelievers, to keep them from seeing the light of the gospel of the glory of Christ, who is the image of God (God of all creation).

2 Corinthians 4:3 (NRSV-CE)
+ (Author's notes in parentheses)

Then another portent appeared in heaven: a great red dragon (Satan), with seven heads and ten horns, and seven diadems on his heads. His tail swept down a third of the stars of heaven (fallen angels called demons) and threw them to the earth. Then the dragon stood before the woman who was about to bear a child, so that he might devour her child as soon as it was born.

Revelation 12:3 - 12:4 (NRSV-CE)
+ (Author's notes in parentheses)

FOREWORD

New Proof of God & Satan is very well-written and includes important insights from credible authors in my profession of Exorcist. Based upon the doctrines of the Catholic Church and my personal experience, I can attest that God, God's angels, Satan, and demons are real and that the Forces of Evil are not a metaphor nor mythology. The book also mentions potential entry points for evil forces made possible by dangerous human behaviors. Modernism has distracted many people from the importance of religious education and practices, and the corresponding lack of faith has had a detrimental effect on them. This book is timely regarding the need for bringing humanity together to solve widely recognized problems.

While I am unable to comment on the author's personal experiences, since they have not yet been formally investigated, the main portions of this book covering societal problems and the author's urging of collaboration towards solutions is commendable.

Father Gary Thomas

Pastor, Sacred Heart Parish

PREFACE TO THE NEW EDITION

This is a divinely inspired nonfiction book that I was compelled to write in 2020, having been informed in late 2019 that a global event would occur in 2020 that would make the public more open to the content. We now know that the global event was the coronavirus COVID-19 pandemic. The research data associated with various topics in the original book is included in this book and is still valid.

One of the goals of this book is to inform the public that the spiritual world is just as important to be aware of as the physical world, since the former has a major impact on the latter. The following is foundational information regarding the war that human beings are born into.

Our world is fundamentally divided into two sides that are at war, Good versus Evil. While different religious faiths have different perspectives, the overwhelming majority accept the realities of the war between Good and Evil. Every human being is born into this war and each human being chooses a side during their lifetime by their actions.

On one side are the God Of All Creation, the spiritual Forces of Good, and good souls working to make our world a better place. On the other side are Satan and the Forces of Evil, including fallen angels (also called demons), additional spiritual entities opposed to God and human beings, and human beings that are doing the work of Satan. We know the aforementioned not only from theology, scriptures, and traditions, but also from the testimony of highly experienced exorcists regarding the many interrogations of and answers from tormented, weakened, and infuriated demons right before they are cast out of their victims.

The ultimate goals of Satan and the Forces of Evil are to destroy human beings, take as many souls hostage to Hell as possible, and to cause as much pain and suffering to human beings as possible. Satan and his minions deceive human beings into believing that they and God do not exist; tempt human beings to commit sins; divide and cause conflict by telepathically implanting thoughts and dreams into human beings in order to trigger counter-productive actions, often utilizing human vanity for the purpose of manipulation; generate controversy through misinformation and lies; and use differences of religion, politics, ethnicity, nationality, and other criteria to inspire human conflict, chaos, violence, and destruction. The highest prevalence of demonic activity is focused on human manipulation towards destructive ends. Examples include: the creation of international military tensions and triggering war; tempting human beings to commit sins; destroying human lives through addictions; and causing human beings to feel so depressed, isolated, and hopeless that they commit suicide.

There is a standard approach used by Satan and his demons to manipulate and control human beings. A demon's typical approach to attacking a human being is to isolate them from supportive relationships in order to make them more vulnerable and weaken their will. Demonic activity might start with infestation (demonic attachment to a location/property that the human being moves into or resides in) or the deliberate targeting of a human being. The typical progression is the following: oppression (targeting a specific individual externally with actions that inspire fear, introduce hardships and afflictions, attacks on relationships, and may entail physical attacks), obsession (entails targeting an individual internally with mental attacks progressing to a critical point when the individual is unable to discern the difference between their own thoughts and those implanted by the demon), and in relatively rare cases, possession (when the demon has complete control of the human being's body and behavior at least some of the time).

A different scenario but more common than many people are aware of is the circumstance of perfect possession, where an individual willingly pledges allegiance to Satan or to a specific demon, and accepts demonic possession in exchange for financial wealth, power, and or other desired benefits.

The key to success for the good souls of this world is to bring humanity together by recognizing that we are all children of God, that we have a responsibility to help each other and to make our world a better place, and that we all have a common enemy in the Forces of Evil. Ideally, we will encourage and help each other, be strong in faith based upon practicing a healthy faith life, and set an honorable example by being the best that we can be each day.

This book encourages a logical and scientific approach to understanding our world and our situation as well as global collaboration among people of all faiths, perspectives, professions, vocations, and experiences. It is imperative that all good souls work together to spread truth, inspire faith, and encourage good works.

When humanity understands the information in this book regarding our war and how demons attack human beings, then many benefits will follow. First, there will be major improvements in human relations. There will also be massive decreases in the following:

1. Social conflicts due to race, heritage, nationality, and politics

2. International political and military tensions

3. The incidence of suicide

4. The incidence of drug overdoses and fatalities

5. The incidence of mass shootings

6. The incidence of violent crime

Benefits will also include unprecedented international collaboration and investment to more effectively and efficiently address existential and other major problems facing humanity, including global warming and climate change, terrorism and cyberterrorism, criminal gangs and drug cartels, slavery, plastics pollution, shortages of antibiotics and vaccines for combatting drug-resistant pathogens, corruption in government and law enforcement, and other problems as well. Progress will be made to improve the quality of life for all, to protect human rights, and to empower people globally in a more prosperous economy of opportunity.

Much has occurred since this book was first published in 2020. According to the World Health organization, to the present date, over seven million people have died from the coronavirus COVID-19. It is rarely a topic on local and national news broadcasts and on news websites. In fact, I get the impression that most of the public does not even think about it, since the coronavirus has become a lot less lethal. I also do not believe that most of the public understands the significance of the pandemic and what it should have taught humanity. Of course, there are major implications for establishing proactive readiness to address future pandemics and a proactive approach to international collaboration for development and distribution of vaccines and testing kits; proactively addressing nationwide and international inventories, supply chains, and logistics for personal protective equipment (PPE), ventilators, and critical medical equipment; and organizations of all types proactively creating business continuity plans and supply chain strategies and contingencies to have in place when the next pandemic or disruptive global event happens.

While there has been endless debate over several theories regarding the evolution of COVID-19, and even unfounded theories of deliberate human involvement, no determination regarding the origin of COVID-19 has been established. One of my concerns is that no one has spoken publicly about the potential of unnatural and deliberate causality. Anyone who reviews several of the documented prophecies throughout history, including Marian encounters at La Salette, Fatima, and Akita, might conclude that either The Great Chastisement of humanity has begun or that a final warning has been provided.

I have attempted to share the most important facts in this book with U.S. government officials; major news media, including U.S. and international broadcasters, newspaper, and website news publishers; specific corporate executives; and a few popular podcasters. While I am surprised that it has taken longer than expected to achieve maximum visibility, I understand that the Forces of Evil are highly motivated to prevent me from exposing them. In fact, the Forces of Evil that I am at war with will lose their advantages over humanity by removing the vail of secrecy around them. I also recognize that it takes great courage for corporate executives to publish facts from this book, which can change the course of human history.

During the past few years, I have learned a lot more information, and have a greater understanding about the mission that I was given, which is called "Bring Humanity Together." The mission was determined long before I learned about it and has had an impact throughout my entire life. Experiences that I previously did not understand or thought I understood, are now viewed with a clear perspective, given the mission assigned to me. This book and the website www.bringhumanitytogether.com are driven by this mission.

AUTHOR'S INTRODUCTION

What does being a secret agent have to do with religion, with proving the existence of God and Satan, and with doing battle against the Forces of Evil? In this case, secrecy is critical to ensure that the secret agent stays alive and acquires compelling life experiences for future testimony, but stays under the radar of our enemies, until the time is right to spring the trap on them. The enemies I am referring to are the enemies of all humanity. In 2015, I was surprised to learn that I was a secret agent for God. In fact, before 2015, I was not even aware of my mission nor God's calling for me. I went through life simply trying to be my best, while trying to understand what was going on around me. What my life adventure has enabled me to achieve, by the grace of God, is to reveal new and compelling proof of the reality of God and Satan, and the very active engagement that the Forces of Good and the Forces of Evil have on human lives on a daily basis. It is my hope that by sharing this critical information, it will result in a significant improvement in how human beings treat each other, inspire a commitment to and practicing of faith that provides protections against evil, and foster unprecedented nationwide and international collaboration to remediate the major problems faced by humanity.

It is my belief that life is sacred, and that each human being is blessed with unique capabilities for contributing to making our world a better place. I also believe that God has a purpose for each of us; and even if it has not yet been revealed to you, tomorrow can be a better day than today.

This book is going to highlight the reality of God and Satan, the reality of the Forces of Good and the Forces of Evil, and what we can do to overcome the challenges and problems that we face. In our increasingly secular world, many people do not realize the sources of adversity that they face. People wonder why the world seems so complicated, why you can try to do everything right, and things still go wrong. Many people also wonder, based upon what they see and hear from the news media and social media, why the world seems to be becoming a more dangerous place. Worse, more people are becoming so habituated to bad news and the crimes and tragedies that are reported on a daily basis, that they have become numb and just accept it as the way things are naturally supposed to be. This leads to a cynicism regarding human behavior, contributes to a lack of trust, introduces problems into communications, and results in increased stress levels as well as interpersonal tensions and conflicts.

One of the things that inspired me to write this book, is that despite all of the books that I have read, and all of the documentaries and videos that I have seen posted on the internet, and countless television broadcasts, I do not see anyone publicly speaking about the vital information included in this book. Specifically, no one that I am aware of is speaking about how prevalent the Forces of Evil are in causing conflict, murder, and mayhem in our world nor how active the Forces of Good are in helping us.

On the contrary, most of the subject matter in books and in videos regarding the Forces of Evil are provided by exorcists with notable insights derived from selflessly helping individuals to be delivered from demonic possession. The people that are possessed against their will, who come to exorcists for help, represent a relatively small percentage of the overall population. In fact, many more people are affected by demonic manipulation and various levels of demonic attack every day. This demonic activity is so widespread that it has a profound impact on the conflicts that we see within our nation as well as conflicts between nations. This is one of the most important revelations of this book.

We are empowered to change our lives and to make our world a safer and better place. There is also great synergy that can be derived through collaboration towards achieving common goals.

It is important to note that I am a messenger and a teacher and not an exorcist nor therapist. I do not provide one-on-one deliverance nor counseling sessions. My responsibility is to share what God has shared with me in terms of vital and helpful information in order to bring humanity together. I do provide interviews and deliver speaking engagements as my schedule permits.

In this book, I have endeavored not to share the actual names of certain people for the purpose of safety as well as to prevent unwanted attention. As you will see, I had no choice but to share my real name.

I hope that this book is a blessing to you, providing enlightenment as well as practical and helpful recommendations. For more information and resources, please visit the website for Bring Humanity Together, LLC at www.bringhumanitytogether.com.

CHAPTER 1: THE GOALS FOR THIS BOOK

The goals for this book are as follows:

1. To share new proof that God and Satan are real.

2. To provide an understanding of Satan's goals and how he and demons affect humanity.

3. To bring humanity together to collaborate against our common enemies.

4. To teach best practices for protecting yourself against the Forces of Evil.

5. To strengthen families, neighborhoods, and communities.

6. To make a call to action for the leaders of every nation and the leaders of every military organization to reassess their views of the world, to de-escalate tensions between nations, and work together to protect the good souls of humanity.

7. To inspire collaboration on an international basis to address urgent problems.

8. To make our world a safer and better place.

I am going to share with you the most important news story of modern times, and it will cause a major intellectual paradigm shift for people all around the globe. While aspects of this news will be distressing and possibly scary for many readers, I want to assure you that there is no need for panic. On the contrary, we need a logical and scientific approach to analyzing this news and applying it to our current situation. I will provide empowering knowledge regarding how to lead a safer and happier life. In fact, if we can get enough human beings to understand and accept what will be new information for many, there are many positive implications for improving our world, including unprecedented international collaboration for addressing existential threats such as climate change, plastics pollution, and the threat of nuclear war; enhancing approaches to mental healthcare and physical healthcare; improving standards and coordination in law enforcement (local, national, international); optimizing strategic and collaborative military focus and investment; enhancing international relationships and trade agreements; and improving and protecting our natural environment and resources.

I want to assure you that the God of all creation is infinitely more powerful than Satan. The Forces of Good are already engaged in protecting the good souls of our world. However, there are behaviors that we can follow to make us safer and to enable us to have a better quality of life. Regardless of whether your religion considers Satan and his demons to be fallen angels, jinn, or other types of entities, we should all accept the fact that they are real, not metaphors, and that they are enemies of mankind. Even if you do not practice a religion today and even if you are an atheist or agnostic, it is to your advantage to learn from this book, and benefit from its recommendations. Not believing in the Forces of Evil does not protect you from them. Not understanding how they affect human beings makes you very vulnerable.

Do not be surprised by this book being publicly reacted to with skepticism. Gabriele Amorth, formerly the Chief Exorcist at the Vatican, lamented in his book, *An Exorcist More Stories*, (Amorth, 2000), that the statistical findings of a study in West Germany were "revealing and terrible", since it found that one third of theologians do not believe in the existence of Satan, and almost two thirds of the theologians that believe in his existence do not believe in his practical actions against humanity and refuse to consider it in pastoral activity.

Of the people that believe Satan is real and the many more that think he might be real, many are under the wrong impression that the Forces of Evil are unable to harm them and the rest of humanity. They might base their belief on the book of Revelation or what they heard about it. Revelation mentions that Satan and a third of the angels were cast out of Heaven down to Earth. Therefore, they are here on Earth with us human beings! As a Catholic, I know that Satan was forever defeated by the crucifixion of Jesus Christ. A deeper explanation of this is provided in Chapter 21 by Father Gabriele Amorth on the centrality of Christ with regard to the plan of creation and redemption. In Revelation, it describes how God and the Forces of Good have already won the war in Heaven. However, individual battles on Earth continue to be lost due to the Forces of Evil and good souls are lost every day. Each of us is responsible for our own behavior; and specific behavior can make us safer, and other behavior can make us vulnerable to the Forces of Evil. This is the reason that there is so much chaos, heartache, and unexpected adversity in many of our lives.

CHAPTER 2: BACKGROUND ON MY SITUATION

My name is Jim, and I believe that I would be described as a middle-aged American with a long and successful career in business and technology consulting, sales, management, and project implementations. I also have a passionate commitment to public service, including serving as an instructor for professional rescuers and civilians at an ambulance squad, as an instructor for civilians at the American Red Cross, and as President of the Central Florida Chapter of HDI, which is a professional association for networking, training, and certifications for the Information Technology Service and Support community.

I am hopeful that my story and what I have learned will be helpful to many people around the world and help millions of people to lead happier lives. This chapter covers recent and relevant experiences. Later in this book, Chapter 21 provides a concise autobiography.

In the Spring of 2006, my second wife, whom I married in 2004, and I decided to relocate from Honey Brook, Pennsylvania, near Philadelphia, to the Orlando, Florida area, where most of her family was. A main reason for relocating to Florida was for my wife's happiness. She wanted to be close to her grown-up children as well as to her elderly mother, who did not have a good support network. She had envisioned her mother would eventually move in with us. I did not have objections to her mother moving into our new home, since she had appeared to be a reasonably agreeable and harmless individual, and my perspective was that this is the normal cycle of life, where many adults end up caring for their elderly parents or elderly close relatives. My children at the time did not object to my moving, since they were very young, living at the home of my first wife, had other places they preferred to be most of the time, and were comfortable with seeing me every couple of weekends, which I was still able to coordinate with my job. They were also excited about having a second home near Disney World. Personally, I was looking forward to beautiful weather and sunshine. My brother and sister that lived within an hour or two of me in Pennsylvania and New Jersey rarely visited me, and most of the time I had to drive to their homes for us to get together.

It was a bit of an ordeal making the trip to Florida. I had completed closing on the new property on December 19th, the day before our move. The bank had made a mistake on the paperwork and for thirty minutes, there was a chance the closing would not happen that day in Orlando, even though I had a flight back to Philadelphia that afternoon. Fortunately, we were able to get the paperwork corrected, but I was physically and emotionally exhausted. My not having slept well the night before, did not help. I got back to my Pennsylvania home late in the day, and my wife and I finished cleaning up the property. We then needed to pack two vehicles with items that could not fit into the large moving company truck, which had already left for Florida the day before. By the time we finished cleaning the house and packing the vehicles, including loading two dogs in her vehicle and two cats in my vehicle, with all animals secured in a protected manner in the passenger seat area, it was 2 AM. We drove all night to get to our new home. My vehicle was so packed that I could not even put my seat back to take a nap. I was tired even before we started driving, so I ended up pumping coffee several times during the drive. When we finally arrived at our new home in Florida the next afternoon, I thought it was a miracle, especially because I had survived. I had never before driven so far a distance. Unfortunately, our vehicles did not have room for several ordinary-looking plants that my wife was emotionally attached to. Therefore, shortly thereafter, I had to drive all her plants to our new home. If that is not an indication of love, I do not know what is. Do not interpret me wrong, because I do appreciate plants, flowers, and nature. I had simply not anticipated the scope of the moving ordeal. My wife and I had been happy together, had good family and social relationships, had good jobs, and both of us felt very blessed upon moving into our newly built home in December of 2006.

Within a few months of relocating to Florida, I unexpectedly experienced a variety of inexplicable challenges and hardships. Starting early in the Spring of 2007, I noticed a negative trend with personal relationships within my local family. Ironically, I was not aware of any new issues nor conflicts. I struggled to understand why the relationships seemed to have more tension.

I could see rising tensions between my wife and her mother, whom had been living alone without much social contact for years, since her husband died in 2001. I typically was the one transporting her mother between our two houses as well as to church, and noticed during these drives with just the two of us, that her mother typically complained about her daughter and her grandchildren, and typically included a token compliment for me. I did not think much about these experiences and simply attributed them to her being elderly, lonely, and needing to vent.

I did not realize that there was much more that needed to be understood about my mother-in-law's personality and state of being, and I was too preoccupied with daily responsibilities to give it more attention. She and her husband had moved from Michigan to retire in Florida in 1993 and had built an active circle of friends that frequently socialized and would go dancing at the local Moose Lodge. The rest of my wife's immediate family soon relocated from Michigan to Florida. My wife's brother with family relocated to Florida soon after the parents, and then my wife moved to Florida in 1997. My wife's two sons had moved into her home by 1999. Unfortunately, my wife's father took ill, and his condition got worse about three years after moving to Florida. He had issues with his feet and the condition seemed to get worse after medical treatment. In fact, my wife and her mother believed that poor medical treatment with inappropriate medication caused his deteriorating health. He developed kidney failure and had to undergo dialysis treatments. He also needed a wheelchair to get around. Gone were the days of dancing with friends and socializing as often as they previously had. Making matters worse, my wife's brother got into financial trouble attempting to purchase and quickly sell a residential property across the street from where he lived, and he needed to sell that house as soon as possible.

My wife's parents agreed to help him by selling their home, which was close to their friends, and to purchase their son's property, which was far from their friends. This decision and relocation resulted in my wife's parents having significantly less time with their friends. My wife's mother experienced the strain of being the sole care giver for her husband, and she grew resentful for the increasing hardships that she was experiencing. She had been so happy when they arrived in Florida and had a very fulfilling social life. Now, most socialization occurred when she attended the church local to her most recent home. Three years later, in 2001, her husband died. My wife and I flew to Florida when we heard her father was close to dying, but he had already passed by the time we arrived at his home. I had not had much time with her father, whom I recall meeting a few months prior. He was very easy-going and a very loving person.

In 2002, my wife moved to Pennsylvania, because she preferred to live with me. It is fair to say that we were very much in love and did not want to be apart. From the moment I met her, I thought my wife was an amazing human being. She is fun to talk to and has a great sense of humor. She has a strong work ethic. She also is exceptionally good at cooking, which is one reason that I am a bigger man because of her! Like me, she enjoys caring for children and pets as well as socializing with family and friends. When she moved to Pennsylvania, she assumed that her brother would look after her mother. It would be two more long years for my wife's mother, before my wife and I relocated to Florida.

My wife and I got married on December 31, 2004, during a vacation in Jamaica. Family and friends wanted to join us, but we needed a romantic vacation, since we had both been traveling a lot for business. I promised everyone that we would invite them to a wedding in the United States. One year later, we got married again in Pennsylvania on December 31, 2005, and had a large family celebration. My wife's mother, sons, and others stayed at our home for a week in Pennsylvania before the wedding. It was a joyous week and celebration. My wife and I were very happy to have both of our families together and it was a special time.

Curiously, as the months went by, my wife and I were told by her mother that my wife's brother, who lived across the street from her, rarely visited her and minimized the amount of time he would interact with her. This sounded very strange to me, but my wife said her brother did not contradict what we were told. I heard that his excuse was that my mother-in-law does not use adequate air conditioning, and it is uncomfortably hot in her home. In retrospect, I infer this means that my mother-in-law's social isolation was virtually absolute and combined with her resentments regarding her decreased quality of life, had a major impact on her. My memories of my wife's mother before my move to Florida were pleasant. When my wife and I would visit, we would go together to a craft fair, go out to dinner, and play dominoes. We generally had a nice time together. I simply considered her mother to be a nice elderly woman. I had not seen a dark side.

Things seemed to change after our move to Florida. The negativity manifested by my mother-in-law seemed to increase with time. She would often stay a weekend a month at my home. Some mornings, she would start the day when she heard me and my wife, by coming out of her bedroom and complaining about my wife. Her negativity increased tension in my home when she would visit, and that tension only increased with time. There did not seem to be any logical reason for the negativity nor the tension that she caused. Within a few months, it became clear to me that I did not want to live in the same house with my mother-in-law. Her presence certainly did not help my relationship with my wife. I remember seeing my mother-in-law's malevolent beady-eyed facial expressions of jealousy when I would be affectionate with my wife. My mother-in-law's social isolation and living conditions must have boosted her resentment of us.

Strangely, my relationship with my wife also seemed to be deteriorating, and the ability for me to have a pleasant conversation with her became progressively more difficult, without explanation. By the end of 2007, she seemed to feel no affection for me. Considering that our entire relationship had been a very loving, physical, and passionate one before the move to Florida, the decreasing affection toward me throughout 2007 was a mystery and I felt helpless to resolve it. In addition, while my wife would frequently join me when I would attend church weekly in Pennsylvania, she acquired an aversion to attending church in Florida in 2007 and beyond. During most of 2007, I perceived there were many reasons why my wife and I should feel blessed, and we should be happy. However, a dark force seemed to have entered into our lives in 2007, and life circumstances got progressively worse. I did not realize it at the time, but the dark force had entered into our lives through someone we trusted. Why am I sharing very personal information with you? The reason is that I want you to know about the harm and life disruptions that the Forces of Evil can do, so that you can protect yourself and those you care about.

In October of 2007, despite being the top revenue producer for my employer and receiving the company's "Outstanding Team Player of the Year Award" that same year, I was abruptly let go without specific nor legitimate reasons. Friends of mine that worked at the same company, including personnel that I had hired, later told me that no details were shared with staff regarding reasons for my departure, and staff were encouraged not to ask about it. What followed was a sequence of difficult jobs over the next thirteen years, and despite notable success in each one of them, there were frequent stressors related to toxicity of the work environment, issues with company management or financial pressures due to earnings challenges. I had not experienced this while living in Pennsylvania.

In 2008, during a drive to take my mother-in-law home after another unpleasant visit to my home, I informed her that I was unwilling to have her move into my home, and she essentially had a temper tantrum and claimed that I was selfish. When I later informed my wife about this, she was not pleased either. Curiously, throughout 2007, when my wife's mother would stay with us, my wife was not very warm to her mother. She would often answer her mother's questions with an angry edge, and this type of interaction continued for years. This edge not only was directed at her mother, but even more so at me and got worse over time.

I have a Bachelor of Science degree from the University of Michigan, and I majored in Psychology because I was eager to understand human behavior, social dynamics, and how to help others. While some social psychologists might explain the changes in my marital relationship as being due to the interactions with a new group of family members that were frequent visitors to my Florida home, I knew there had to be much more going on. From my viewpoint, my behavior, responsibilities, and daily routine had not changed significantly from when I lived in Pennsylvania. I worked hard at the same job, which I had enjoyed. I put my wife, family, pets, and other loved ones first. The home that I lived in was newly built for me in 2006, and the development where it is had been the previous site of citrus orchards, so I did not perceive or even consider anything negative associated with my new home from a paranormal standpoint. In fact, the new home was beautiful and felt comfortable in every way. While life circumstances progressively seemed to fall apart around me, I had no clue why. I would later learn the specific reasons why.

In 2008, my wife and I went through our longest periods of unemployment before getting back into the workforce in 2009. Neither of us had experienced any significant amount of time unemployed before moving to Florida. Later, in September of 2009, after I perceived my wife's treatment of me had deteriorated to the point of becoming intolerably rude, I told her that I would rather get a divorce than continue to live together, unless fundamental respect and consideration could be restored. She shook her head affirmatively about things needing to change, surprisingly responding in an uncharacteristic unemotional way, and it seemed to trigger a recalibration, whereby the rudeness greatly decreased, although living together continued to be more of a cohabitation with shared chores responsibilities. I had been heartbroken for some time, not knowing why nor how our relationship got to where it was and feeling helpless to improve it. My wife was never willing to discuss it. In addition, while my wife's family relationships were not adversely affected during this time, her family seemed to progressively adopt my wife's attitude toward me, and the emotional distance with me increased quickly over time. I perceived that I was helpless to change this.

In late 2009, shortly after that pivotal discussion with my wife, God started communicating to me in a consistent manner. He told me that there is a reason that I am suffering and that I should stand firm, continue to do the best I can, and to stay in the marriage, because a much larger responsibility was coming to me in the future. God proceeded to point things out to me, which I had not noticed before, and to share knowledge that is not available in any books. God explained to me what had happened and why my life seemed to unravel after moving to Florida. In summary, my wife's mother had become possessed before our move to Florida. To me, this would explain why my wife's brother minimized his time with his mother. Once he saw her dark side, which I got to see in progressively more menacing ways, I can understand why he would decrease contact. This also may explain why my mother-in-law would mention on several occasions that she had a new "great friend" that would come and see her as well as take her shopping and also to church, but then suddenly no longer be in her life.

Human beings naturally need some level of positive social interaction. Complete social isolation has been long known to be harmful, for both psychological and physical health reasons. Isolation is the typical strategy used by the demonic because it weakens the human's self-esteem and will to fight. For people that do not understand that thoughts in their minds can be planted by demonic forces, they are at great risk of manipulation. If people are desperately lonely, a demon can even pretend to be their friend, revealing itself after getting the person to embrace several thoughts that they have planted and watching their physical signs of agreement. Demons can see us, but most humans are unable to see them. Demons cannot read minds, but they are capable of deductive reasoning and can see responses of humans to their actions and the thoughts that they plant. Combine this with thousands of years of experience afflicting and tormenting human beings, which each demon has, and you can understand why demons are formidable. In some cases, a human being willingly submits to a demon and welcomes possession in exchange for power, wealth, or other desired rewards. For someone that is extremely lonely, the reward desired might be friendship. This situation of human willful submission to a demon and possession is called "perfect possession." God told me that due to extreme loneliness, longstanding resentments, and a desire to be able to cause harm, that my mother-in-law became perfectly possessed prior to my relocation to Florida.

On the other hand, possessed people that are unwilling victims seek help from exorcists to be freed from suffering that disrupts their lives. These victims may have become possessed as a result of involvement in occult activities, they may have been targeted and afflicted through witchcraft, they may have been dedicated to Satan while they were infants or children by malevolent parents or relatives, and there may be other reasons as well. There are many cases in which people are possessed due to no fault of their own. Exorcism is a ritual of healing deliverance.

Fortunately, God's grace provided emotional support to me and God also bestowed upon me spiritual faculties, which are called charisms. These charisms enable me to perceive things that I could not perceive beforehand. Charisms are mentioned in Holy Scripture.

For years, I have had the unusual capability to physically feel God's grace; and even though I have spoken to many clergy about it, and I have not yet met anyone else that experiences similar physical manifestations of the presence of God. Christians and other believers in God are wisely taught to walk by faith and Holy Scripture, and to not be guided by physical feelings nor supernatural signs. However, I was now receiving God's guidance and teachings directly, which were consistent with Holy Scripture, and I was growing stronger in faith and capabilities. Instead of having only five senses, I was eventually blessed with at least ten, since there are spiritual counterparts to our physical senses, in addition to others. One of the charisms I received enables me to see when people are possessed by demons, including the case of my mother-in-law. To this day, when

I am in a public place, especially when there is a large quantity of people, it is not uncommon that I will notice at least two people that look at me with great fear, and at least one person that looks at me with great anger and sometimes fear as well. None of those people know me, but their demons do. During these years in Florida, it was almost like being in a movie where several people, except me, knew who I was and God's destiny for me.

Having been granted new capabilities of perception and awareness by God, I started to notice more of my mother-in-law's malevolent micro-expressions. My mother-in-law also demonstrated dramatic and spontaneous changes in physical capabilities. At most times, her attempt to walk even short distances with a cane was shaky, and she would appear very unsteady. With her free hand, she often grabbed onto nearby counters and furniture as she moved. However, at other times, when my wife was not in the same room, I saw my mother-in-law walk briskly, quietly, and with great agility, like someone more in her twenties than in her actual age of middle 80s and later her low 90s. To me, she also gave off a very creepy vibe. She seemed to like hovering behind me and other people, especially when they were watching television. During 2015, while she would stay at my home at my wife's insistence, my mother-in-law would aggressively approach me on several occasions when my wife was not in the same room, and verbalize disturbing things, all the while exhibiting her malevolent expressions. My wife did not believe my concerns, nor did she understand why for years I would lock our bedroom door when her mother would stay overnight, even though I did not lock the door when any other relatives or friends stayed overnight. I was encouraged by God to remain faithful and steadfast, because "something big" in terms of a new responsibility was now coming my way soon.

CHAPTER 3: GOD ENGAGES ME TO DECEIVE SATAN

God came up with a plan to deceive Satan into revealing himself to me in a way that I can reveal him to the rest of humanity. God devised the plan based upon his experience and knowledge of Satan's boundless vanity. God engaged me without informing me regarding the details of the plan, possibly to make sure that I did not accidentally divulge information to any other human beings or to Satan, and probably to make my testimony more credible. Instead, in 2015, God convinced me through his grace and guidance that he was developing me to be able to provide spiritual guidance, deliverance, and exorcism. He directed me to notify the local Catholic Diocese of Orlando regarding my interest and capabilities for helping people within the nine counties that the Diocese serves. I did not give much thought to the fact that I was married, had not attended seminary, etc. I simply desired to be obedient to God. Two days after I visited the diocesan exorcist, Satan made an audacious threat to me in the form of a digital photograph. He felt safe doing this because my revealing the photograph would also reveal my name, which is in the photograph, and put my life and potentially others in danger. In retrospect, that threat was meant not as much for 2015 as it is for now in 2020. As I look back on my life, I believe that God long ago had established a destiny for my life, and Satan may have known at least that it had huge implications. The hardships and afflictions that I have experienced over the years must have been for the purpose of discouraging me from fulfilling my destiny. Satan's initial threat in the photograph and subsequent, unprecedented actions, were clearly aimed at discouraging me from offering to help other people as well as to prevent me from revealing him to humanity. Satan has underestimated God, underestimated humanity, and underestimated me.

Starting in the Spring of 2015, I was guided by God to learn more about combatting the Forces of Evil as well as the rite of exorcism. With increasing frequency, I experienced physical manifestations of the presence of God in the form of grace and streams of encouraging thoughts when watching movies, interviews, and reading subject matter regarding the deliverance of suffering people through the rite of exorcism. Considering my mother-in-law, and what I had experienced since 2007, this topic was very relevant to my personal life. My experiences of God's grace became intense. This caused me to believe that I was undergoing a type of spiritual anointing. In fact, these experiences became so frequent and distracting from my normal daily duties, that I felt compelled to follow God's directions and schedule a meeting on June 19th with the Chancellor for Canonical Affairs and Vicar General for the Diocese of Orlando for the purpose of offering to help the Diocese of Orlando with spiritual counseling and exorcism. I had anticipated that I would be expected to help any of the two and a half million people in the metropolitan area of Orlando, both Catholic and non-Catholic, after going through some type of vetting and mentoring process. Through my research, I learned that, depending upon the specific Catholic diocese, 40 – 60% of people that ask for spiritual deliverance and or an exorcism are not

Catholic. Generally speaking, in the United States and around the world, regardless of religion, people seeking spiritual deliverance are often turned away, simply because the local clergy do not believe in demons or choose not to practice exorcism. Today in the year 2020, there are entire countries where an afflicted person is unable to obtain an exorcism.

I experienced a surreal feeling during my drive to the Vicar General's office, realizing that I was probably the only lay person to ever make this type of offer. I also had no one to discuss what I was being compelled to do, because I did not have anyone close to me that could understand a spiritual matter, such as this. Many of the people that I know are agnostic in terms of faith and manifest a confused expression if the topic of possession in real life is brought up.

The Chancellor for Canonical Affairs and Vicar General has a very commanding presence, and he is very cordial. When I told him that I perceived that God seemed to be developing me to be an exorcist, he immediately suggested an introduction to the Bishop-appointed exorcist for the Diocese of Orlando. In general, diocesan exorcists are typically not listed publicly on websites nor in telephone directories, in order not to attract the wrong types of attention. There are a lot of people that may think that they are afflicted by a demon but may have psychological or medical issues that cause them to feel that way. There is typically a stringent vetting process to rule out natural causes before someone is referred to a diocesan exorcist. At the end of our meeting, I did in fact confirm with the Vicar General that he had never heard of a lay person ever making the type of offer that I did.

On July 8th, I was able to meet with the exorcist for the Diocese of Orlando. While I offered to help the priest with the ministry, he emphasized to me the burden of this responsibility, given that he had so many other pressing duties. He also mentioned that he only did exorcisms during weekday hours, which was while I had other day job responsibilities, so that was an obstacle for me to join him for any assistance and mentoring opportunities. This devoted priest could not have been more welcoming and candid, and he had a vast amount of knowledge to share. In fact, he was so forthcoming and expressive, that I mainly listened and did not share details of my personal spiritual experiences, challenges, nor perceived charisms and faculties. Consequently, my offer to assist the priest was interpreted as simply offering value regarding discernment, due to my degree in Psychology from the University of Michigan, and my capabilities to secure the environment (that is, employing physical restraint, if needed) due to my athletic appearance.

CHAPTER 4: THE PHOTOGRAPH – SATAN'S THREAT IS REVEALED!

Exactly two days later, on July 10th, 2015, while in my home office, I was cleaning and reorganizing my office in advance of starting a new job. I decided to photograph four modest awards on my desk that I had received from my most recent employer, and then I planned to store the awards out of sight in a cabinet. The awards were on the left side of my desk, and to ensure that I was not in any reflection, I held my smartphone far to the left of me. After I took the photograph with my Apple iPhone, I viewed the photograph and noticed several features that were fascinating from a scientific standpoint.

When you first look at the photograph, you will see the four clear resin paper weights with inscriptions, including my name and other data on each one. As you look toward the right side of the photograph, you notice that there are images within the lower right and upper right awards. When you take a closer look at the lower right, you will notice a humanoid face with a distinct right eye that appears to be looking at the awards. That was my first impression. However, if you focus on that right eye while you zoom in, you will notice that the humanoid face is looking at you, the photograph viewer. More facial features, including nose, mouth, and a goat like beard also become apparent. If you look further down, below the face, you can identify a dark shaded object that appears to be a four-prong pitchfork, which is firmly gripped by what appears to be a reddish right hand. It is at this point you can recognize the distinct iconography of Satan. I realize that spiritual beings are shape shifters, but Satan is the epitome of evil, an evil despot, who micromanages his vast army of demons. You can be certain that he is the most horrible of horrible bosses. Based upon research, we know that Satan and his demons are all fallen angels, and similar to the angels in Heaven, they are organized by rank in a very structured manner, just as Holy Scripture describes heavenly angels organized into nine choirs. Therefore, even though demons are known to frequently lie, none of them would dare impersonate their boss, Satan. By the way, there are multiple other features within the photograph, including multiple demons, and the ability of the image of Satan to appear to morph into the image of a woman, if your point of focus is on the left eye. Do not let it disturb you, it is only a photograph, and the threat is directed at me.

The upper right portion of the photograph may be a little more difficult for some people to see. If you notice the smooth rounded shadowy edges, it will be easier to notice that you are looking at the tops of a collection of multiple skulls personified with angry expressions. In real life, skulls do not show expressions of emotion; therefore, the expression of anger is part of Satan's overall message to me. In most cultures, skulls mean death. Therefore, when you combine the iconography of Satan with the message of death, you can deduce that this is a deliberate threat to me. While I was surprised when I first recognized what was in the photograph, I was not scared. I was already strong in my faith in God and knew that Satan and demons existed. On the contrary, I found the photograph to be fascinating from a scientific standpoint, extremely compelling, and very valuable to help other people believe, since no other photograph of Satan has ever been taken.

An important question came to mind, "Why would Satan threaten a mortal human being?" Satan and his demons are responsible for countless deaths and chaos every day. What can he possibly be threatened by or afraid of? Clearly, Satan was not happy that I met with a church official and clergy. He was also not pleased that I was offering to help many people to be protected from his attacks. Would this be sufficient incentive for Satan to reveal himself for the first time in human history in a visual artifact? Many saints have suffered afflictions from Satan, and these are described in their autobiographies and biographies. However, Satan has not threatened them in a manner that created undeniable, visible, permanent proof.

The nature of the threat is also interesting, since a human being is typically not capable of fighting directly with a demon for multiple reasons. A demon cannot be injured nor destroyed by physical weapons nor physical attacks, because a demon is a spiritual being. In addition, a demon, unlike a human being, does not depend upon sleep nor human food, has the "wisdom of the ages", including thousands of years of experience studying and warring against human beings, and does not have the mortality nor weaknesses that human beings have. In fact, for all of us human beings that battle demons, all of our manifested power against evil comes directly from God and God's angels. All glory goes to God. There is no room for human vanity while fighting evil.

Going back to my question, "Why would Satan threaten a mortal human being?" If you were in an army at war, and you could defeat your enemy in front of you on the battlefield, in most cases, you probably would choose to defeat your enemy and not take the time to threaten them. Therefore, Satan must have known that he and his demons would not be able to harm me. This would later be proven on multiple occasions. In fact, there have been at least three occasions where they attempted to take my life and failed because of God's protection. Satan even attempted to intimidate me by speaking directly to me in a threatening and taunting manner on two occasions, in early morning hours, through a baby monitor located near my bed and by further defying the limitations of technology by invading two conference calls that I had for my professional association without any record of Satan "dialing in." I have kept detailed records by date and time to keep track of my adventure, and I look forward to sharing more details.

In addition, why would Satan take the risk of losing his most important weapon, specifically the secrecy of his Forces of Evil, and the fact that many human beings do not believe in him? Clearly, Satan deemed me a large enough risk to take such a desperate action. Satan's appearance in the photograph is very audacious and is consistent with his personality. He knew that I could not go public without risking all aspects of my life, since my name is on the awards in the photo. One film director that I spoke to suggested concealing my name on the photograph. I responded that credibility is most important and modifying the photograph in any manner may introduce doubt for a potentially skeptical public. In terms of actual danger, while I have been shown that I have nothing to fear from Satan and his demons, there will always be the potential threat of evil human beings in this nation and around the world that are disciples of Satan. In fact, these people are a threat to everyone that is not a disciple of Satan.

Satan had probably based his decision of revealing himself on most of the human beings that he has known throughout history, thinking it unlikely that a human being would risk ruining their own life and even death in order to help other human beings. On the other hand, Satan's vanity and rage may have gotten the better of him, and without thinking, he chose to expose himself believing there would be no significant consequences. Over thousands of years, it is possible for even Satan to make a mistake. In retrospect, I believe that Satan's threat to me in 2015, and his others since then, were all for the purpose of discouraging me from revealing the reality of Satan and demons to you and the rest of humanity in 2020.

In the film, "Hostage To The Devil", 2016, directed by Marty Stalker, Laurene Gomez MA, LMFT states that it is difficult to convince the public that Satan is real, because we do not have any visual evidence, such as a photograph to point to. I am very pleased to say that now we do have one!

The purpose for the following website URL is to enable owners of the hardback and paperback versions of the book *New Proof of God & Satan* to have access to the digital version of the photograph described in this Chapter 4, which is easier to analyze in digital format than the printed format.

To view the digital version of the photograph and analyses, you can visit this website URL: https://www.bringhumanitytogether.com/the-photograph/.

Please keep in mind that the photograph was taken with an older Apple iPhone with a much lower resolution than current smartphones. Also, if I had known in advance that these images would have been in the photograph, I would have used a higher-resolution camera. Furthermore, the features of the photographs are easier to see and analyze in their color electronic formats, because of the capability to zoom in and out as well as the RGB and projected light aspect of a monitor as opposed to the characteristics of printed photographs.

CHAPTER 5: THE IMPORTANCE OF A LASTING VISUAL PROOF OF SATAN

Why is it so important to have lasting visual proof of Satan? I infer that the answer is that most humans rely on sight for learning and for evidence. A large body of written works, documentaries, and video testimonials that mention evidence of Satan's works do not seem to be enough to convince the majority of human beings. The age-old expression is "Seeing is believing." As irrational as it seems to me, some people have even told me their naïve desire to experience demonic attack personally in order to validate for themselves that demons exist. Another age-old expression is "Be careful what you wish for." What is important is that the implications of the proof I am sharing affect everyone's life, regardless of religion and current belief system.

While an event with compelling visual phenomena will convince a percentage of people that what they are seeing is real, it probably will not convince everyone, especially skeptics that are already committed to disbelief. Furthermore, many human beings today tend to have short attention spans, partly due to the information overload we experience on a daily basis, and memories from any event that happens usually fades quickly over time, unless the event is traumatizing or has lasting effects.

Take for example, a miracle sighted back on October 13, 1917, when, by some accounts, over seventy thousand people gathered in a large field in Fátima, Portugal in order to witness a prophesied miracle. They had gathered there because ten year old Lúcia de Jesus Rosa dos Santos, who later became a nun known globally as Sister Lúcia, had told everyone that the Blessed Virgin Mary committed to appearing to her that day, and that a miracle of God was going to take place for all of the people to see.

Prior to this, beginning in the spring of 1917, at Cova da Iria, in Fátima, Portugal, three young sheep herding children, including Lúcia and her two cousins Francisco de Jesus Marto and his sister Jacinta de Jesus Marto, reported seeing apparitions of an Angel. Then starting on May 13, 1917, and over the subsequent five consecutive months, apparitions of the Blessed Virgin Mary appeared to them. Lúcia's reports of the visions received global attention. In fact, newspaper reporters, photographers, clergy from the Roman Catholic Church, many townspeople, and many visitors from other countries came to witness the proceedings.

What occurred on October 13, 1917 became known as the "Miracle of the Sun". As Jeffrey S. Bennett described in *When the Sun Danced: Myth, Miracles, and Modernity in Early Twentieth-Century Portugal* (Bennett, 2012), after a period of rain, the dark clouds broke and the Sun appeared as an opaque, spinning disc in the sky. It was said to be significantly duller than normal, allowing everyone to look at it directly, and to cast multicolored lights across the landscape, the people, and the surrounding clouds. The Sun was then reported to have careened towards the Earth before zigzagging back to its normal position. Father John De Marchi, an Italian Catholic priest and researcher who wrote several books on the subject, which included descriptions by witnesses who believed they had seen a miracle created by Mary, Mother of God, in *The True Story of Fátima* (De Marchi, 1952), mentions that witnesses reported that their previously wet clothes became "suddenly and completely dry, as well as the wet and muddy ground that had been previously soaked because of the rain that had been falling." In addition, the three children reported seeing visions during the event.

The quantity of annual visitors to Fátima's holy sites is a testament to how important it continues to be for many people of faith. In February of 2020, officials at the Marian Shrine of Fátima said 6.3 million pilgrims visited the famed site in central Portugal in 2019, which compares with a range over the past decade of between 4 million to 9.4 million pilgrims visiting per year.

The following photographs are associated with the events described at Fátima and current venues:

Lúcia Santos, Francisco Marto, and Jacinta Marto

An image of the crowd during the Miracle of the Sun
on October 13, 1917

Page from Ilustração Portuguesa, October 29, 1917,
showing the people looking at the Sun during the
Miracle of the Sun on October 13, 1917

Monument of the Guardian Angel of Portugal apparition
to the three little shepherd children

Three Little Shepherds monument

Fátima Main Square

Chapel of the Apparitions

The devotion to Our Lady of Fátima

A religious statue depicting the Immaculate
Heart of Mary as described by Sister Lúcia

While the events at Fátima have important meaning to millions of people today, why, in a world of 7.8 billion people, is the reality of God and a discernable impact on human behaviors not more visible in our daily news? Why is there such a lack of faith, so much conflict, and so many counterproductive behaviors, both within nations and between nations?

My point is that a miraculous event at an instant in time, even when followed by miraculous healings for pilgrims to that site over the years, only receives limited visibility among humanity. However, if there is a lasting and compelling artifact, such as a photograph that can be studied by experts, including theologians, clergy, photographers, scientists, and others, then that photograph and the objective research findings can be spread quickly around the world via broadcast news, social media, and other means to reach billions of people. That is what we need to happen as soon as possible regarding the first photograph of Satan. If most people recognize that all of us have an extremely dangerous common enemy, it will make it much easier for all of us to live together in harmony and become a unified front as well as to collaborate to remediate other important problems.

Another benefit of having a lasting visual artifact of Satan is that it enables people to understand a very important truth: you ultimately get paid by who you work for. By this, I am presenting a simple analogy: just like your employer pays you for the hours you work for that employer, you will be paid during and after your life based upon your life's work either by God or by Satan. Specifically, your future will be controlled either by God or by Satan, depending upon whether you have been doing God's work or if you have been doing Satan's work. As soon as someone realizes that God and Satan are real, they have an urgent and vested interest in consciously making certain that they are deliberately working for whom they choose. Lack of belief, lack of knowledge, lack of wisdom, and lack of sense does not protect anyone. No one is allowed excuses. There are only two sides in this war and you either serve God and support the Forces of Good or you serve Satan and support the Forces of Evil. In summary, if you choose to do evil, your future will be much more agonizing than the worst thing that you ever do to another human being. If you choose to live life as a good soul, being the best that you can be and helping others, your future will be even better than today. You may be familiar with this:

> But the path of the righteous is like the light of dawn,
> which shines brighter and brighter until full day.
> The way of the wicked is like deep darkness;
> they do not know over what they stumble.

Proverbs 4:18 – 4:19 (NRSV-CE)

I previously mentioned the expression "Seeing is believing." What I have found is that "Believing is seeing." To be more specific, I have found that as your faith in God increases, and as your belief in the reality of a spiritual world increases, your ability to see and perceive what is going on around you dramatically increases. This larger perspective helps increase your level of human compassion. It also enables you to respond instead of reacting when people act in an inappropriate manner or in an uncharacteristic way. By recognizing that the other person is also a child of God that may be affected by negative experiences earlier in the day, by personal hardships, and perhaps by a tragedy, it enables you to better analyze the interaction and to respond thoughtfully as opposed to react emotionally. In other circumstances, it can help you discern attempts by malevolent people to deceive you. In summary, developing a strong faith enhances your ability to perceive what is going on in your world, and also fortifies a positive attitude, both of which yield many benefits and opportunities.

CHAPTER 6: MY PERSONAL TRANSFORMATION

In order to fulfill God's calling for me, I learned that I needed to completely transform my priorities and commit myself to the greater good. For much of my adult life, I simply tried to be the best husband and father that I could be, to perform at a high level at work, to conduct lifelong learning to improve my skills, and to give back in some way to society. I lived my life on a relatively small stage, in my humble opinion. I never pursued fame nor was particularly active in social media.

This new mission entails more responsibilities and new challenges. Prayer and the Holy Spirit have made this transformation easier, but that does not mean that it has been easy. In fact, the transformation required enormous patience and faith, because it took years to prepare before going public. Not having clergy to confide in, due to potential risk if my information was released too soon, nor a significant other to confide in, made this mission begin on a lonely and arduous path. Between the end of 2015 and now, being required to endure aspects of my life situation, which provided no encouragement nor emotional support, was also taxing. The personal commitment required for this mission entails always being prepared to confront the Forces of Evil, both inhuman and human, since there is no possibility for me of getting off of the battlefield. It also entails a commitment to a high level of responsible living and always being ready to help others in danger.

In essence, the commitment entails self-restraint, discipline, never-ending training, vigilance, valor, and humility. All of this is in preparation for life in the public eye and on the world stage that will be very different from the celebrity recognition enjoyed by athletes, musicians, directors and actors, and politicians. My mission is to bring humanity together, to inspire unprecedented harmony and collaboration within the United States, and also inspire unprecedented collaboration between nations to support each other for the benefit of humanity as well as to confront and dominate the Forces of Evil.

I am a messenger and a teacher and getting mankind to be noble, "take the high road", and leave past conflicts, tragedies, and heartbreaks in the past, will not be a small undertaking. There are too many human beings weighed down with resentments, prejudicial views, and distrust for others. Why am I asking them and all of us to commit to a new life of harmony and collaboration? The reason is that God is giving mankind the chance to save an enormous number of lives that will be lost if we do not start working together to create a better world for all. Intelligent people know that violence begets more violence, war, and suffering. Scholars as well as anyone who studies history should be able to see the tragedies of people that have not learned the lessons of history. We have a lot of history that we can learn from. Let us focus our efforts on living in peace, demonstrating wisdom, and working together for a brighter future.

As a result of my transformation, I have noticed interesting changes. Since 2015, photographs of me can have significant and unusual attributes. Redactions are to protect the identity of others. In this photograph, there is nothing above me except a clear blue sunny sky:

Beginning in 2015, I noticed a new, distinctive, and persistent "X" mark that appears on my forehead. I have never heard anyone mention it and it usually does not show up in photographs or in videos. However, when I was at the HDI Annual Conference in 2016 and nominated for the Local Chapter Officer of the Year Award, it appeared crystal clear to me on multiple large projection screens. No worries for any Harry Potter novel series fans, the mark has nothing to do with Lord Voldemort.

I believe that the significance of this mark is at least twofold: i.e. that I am "one of the good guys", and second, I am blessed with God's favor.

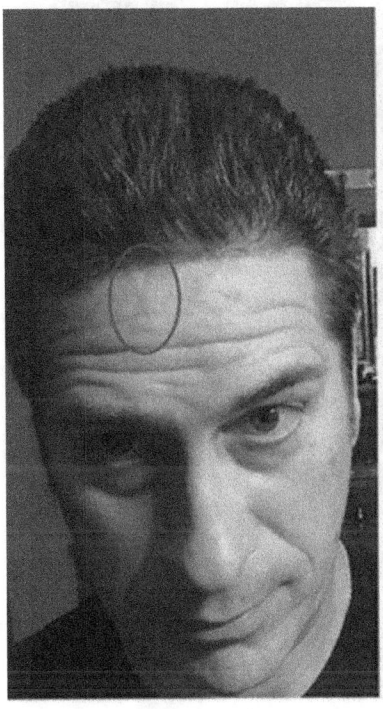

Sometimes, the mark will have a more dramatic appearance:

I believe that the mark is scriptural, and the following are references in the Old Testament and New Testament that may be relevant:

> Now the glory of the God of Israel had gone up
> from the cherub on which it rested to the
> threshold of the house. The Lord called
> to the man clothed in linen, who had the
> writing case at his side; and said to him,
> "Go through the city, through Jerusalem,
> and put a mark on the foreheads of those
> who sigh and groan over all the abominations
> that are committed in it." To the others he
> said in my hearing, "Pass through the city
> after him, and kill; your eye shall not
> spare, and you shall show no pity. Cut
> down old men, young men and young
> women, little children and women, but
> touch no one who has the mark. And
> begin at my sanctuary."

Ezekiel: Chapter 9: 3 – 9:6 (NRSV-CE)

After this I saw four angels standing at the four
corners of the earth, holding back the four winds
of the earth so that no wind could blow on earth
or sea or against any tree. I saw another angel

ascending from the rising of the sun, having
the seal of the living God, and he called with
a loud voice to the four angels who had been
given power to damage earth and sea, saying,
"Do not damage the earth or the sea or the trees,
until we have marked the servants of our
God with a seal on their foreheads."

Revelation: Chapter 7:1 – 7:3 (NRSV-CE)

And the fifth angel blew his trumpet, and I saw a
star that had fallen from heaven to earth, and he
was given the key to the shaft of the bottomless
pit; he opened the shaft of the bottomless pit, and
from the shaft rose smoke like the smoke of a great
furnace, and the sun and the air were darkened
with the smoke from the shaft. Then from the
smoke came locusts on the earth, and they were
given authority like the authority of scorpions
of the earth. They were told not to damage the
grass of the earth or any green growth or any
tree, but only those people who do not
have the seal of God on their foreheads.

Revelation: Chapter 9:1 – 9:4 (NRSV-CE)

Then I looked, and there was the Lamb,
standing on Mount Zion! And with him
were one hundred forty-four thousand
who had his name and his Father's name
written on their foreheads.

Revelation: Chapter 14:1 (NRSV-CE)

While going through this adventure, I have noticed the following:

- I sense a stronger connection with nature and have had and continue to have frequent and unusual interactions with assorted wildlife. Here are a couple of examples. For most months of the year, every time I go outside, I am visited by dragonflies. Sometimes there are multiple that approach me, but they always fly and or land close enough to me to ensure I see them. My home is not far from a small, forested area, but for most of my life, seeing dragonflies has been fairly rare. Even for most years that I have lived in Florida, I did not see them virtually all of the time, like I have seen them since 2015. Even if I am driving on a busy street or a highway with traffic lights, in relatively urban areas far from any parks and forest, often I will see them near my windshield, such as when I am stopped at a traffic light. There are many postings to be seen on internet search engines, with most posts suggesting my experiences are related to on-going and future transformation, encouraging living in the moment and getting the most out of life, connection to loved ones who have passed away, and connection to the spirit world. Perhaps more prayer will provide a deeper understanding.

I also had a very unusual experience back in 2014. On Friday, April 25th, around 5:40 PM, I was driving home from work and was within a couple of miles from my exit. Traffic was surprisingly light for rush hour. I noticed the unusual sight of a solitary bird directly in front of me over two miles ahead. After I passed a highway sign indicating my exit was now one mile away, I noticed that the bird was still flying towards me, was a lot closer, and was closing fast on me. As it approached, I could see that it was very large for a bird, had distinctive raptor features, and the reddish feathers of a hawk. It seemed to be looking at me and flying straight at my face. I looked straight left, right, upwards, and in my rear-view mirrors, but I could not see any possible prey that this hawk was pursuing. I also still did not see any other birds in the sky, which made the situation a little surreal. The large hawk flew right at me at my level in front of my windshield with talons open and so close that I could see the striations of its feathers. I marveled at how impressive the bird looked in attack mode. Just as the hawk got within a few feet in front of my windshield, I checked traffic quickly and swerved my vehicle at the last second in order to avoid injuring it. I had never had an experience like this before.

That evening, around 2 AM, I woke up with the worst sore throat I have ever had. I took some medication and was able to get through the night. After awakening the next morning, I noticed that I still had a sore throat, and my uvula was swollen to the point that it was blocking the back of my throat. I inferred from research online that I had come down with strep throat from a co-worker. Earlier in the week, an office co-worker had asked me for technical support, because she was having difficulty with software on her laptop. I dutifully remediated her technical issues, only to hear her speak two hours later about how she had spent time during the previous weekend in a hospital suffering from strep throat. In retrospect, the experience with the hawk was meant to be a clear warning.

- I noticed a stronger connection with the spiritual world. My abilities to perceive good and evil have been enhanced, even when the latter presents itself in disguise, and my abilities to combat evil have been strengthened as well. I also acquired the ability to have lucid dreams, recognize when I was dreaming, and notice any anomalous features of dreams. I would routinely have positive interactions with loved ones who have passed away. I also had notable visitations by various demonic entities, especially succubae, which would get frustrated by my recognizing and denying them, and then they would come back other times highly disguised. Satan rarely would reveal himself in a dream, but if he did, his presence was always very short, because I would immediately counter with binding prayers. I would either spontaneously wake up speaking the prayers or my wife would wake me up by complaining that I woke her up by speaking in my sleep.

- God shares wisdom and important points with me on a daily basis and even occasionally clarifies relevant news items for me. This attention and interaction have helped sustain me through unbelievable challenges over the years. I have no ego in this adventure, and I welcome all of the assistance that I can get.

CHAPTER 7: DEMONIC INTIMIDATION AFTER THE PHOTOGRAPH

The following are examples of progressively increasing intimidation that Satan has been responsible for. Needless to say, it has not been fun. This adventure has required a great deal of courage, faith, and patience. While the frequency of spiritual annoyances has decreased dramatically at the time of this book writing, between the end of 2015 and 2019, these are some of the intimidating actions that took place:

- Fire alarms that would spontaneously beep three times in the middle of the night without natural cause. This occurred only after relocating to Florida and has occurred multiple times. I always replace batteries yearly. What is even more unusual is that this activity occurred even after I replaced the original standard fire alarms in 2016 with fire alarms that actually verbalize which one is activated and explain whether the danger is smoke, fire or carbon monoxide. However, during these detector activations, only three beeps were heard, which is different from their standard operation, which I tested after each battery installation. The three beeps detector activations would continue every few months after midnight in the early hours of the morning. Each time, I inferred that it was the typical demonic activity of mocking the Holy Trinity.

- There were a few occasions when my home security alarm would emit a deactivation warning beep after midnight, alerting me to the issue. I would check out the system and see no electrical problems. I even had multiple personnel from the security monitoring company do testing and review logs. Each time they could see the exact time of deactivation but had no explanation for how it could be deactivated without my deliberate effort.

- Demonic visitations and intimidations in dreams increased until I became more proficient at efficiently vanquishing them while they were happening.

- The Christmas Season of 2015 was not a joyful time for me, due to my evil mother-in-law. For years, my wife did not care about my concerns regarding her nor that I did not even want her mother in our home. This was the sequence of events.

On November 24th, just before Thanksgiving, my wife brought her mother to stay overnight, since she was to travel the next day to visit relatives in Michigan. The next morning, my mother-in-law tried to start an argument with me, but I refused to indulge her. That Friday, one of my beloved pugs, Dolly, had an Ophthalmologist appointment. The doctor did a blood test and was so alarmed after seeing the results that she insisted that Dolly be taken to her veterinarian on Monday. At the time, Dolly was ten years old, which is two years younger than the typical lifespan of a pug. She seemed as happy as ever. Dolly had been very healthy her entire life and had not shown any signs of distress nor serious health problems ever before. That Sunday, my mother-in-law returned from Michigan and my wife planned to have her stay at our home for a few days. The next day, after a veterinary examination and testing, Dolly was diagnosed with a rare and often fatal autoimmune disorder called Evan's Syndrome. This was terrible news, but our veterinarian, Dr. Stroud, thought there was medication and a treatment regimen to help Dolly. That evening, my mother-in-law barged into my office, got in my face, and with a mocking and evil countenance said, "Are you going to bless Dolly with holy water?" The next evening, Dolly awoke from a nightmare at 3:10 AM and had trouble catching her breath for forty minutes. Her condition seemed worse when my mother-in-law was in my home.

I had been anxious about my wife's plan to bring her mother to our home for several days before Christmas, since during her prior visit, she seemed more aggressive toward me about engaging in unpleasant conversation, always when my wife was not in the room. My mother-in-law had a malevolent look, and I perceived her having glowing red pupils during each one-on-one conversation with me. If you ever see someone with glowing red pupils, you can be sure their problem cannot be remedied by an ophthalmologist. Dolly had just had a better week and seemed to be improving. I was worried that my mother-in-law's visit could have a negative impact.

On Monday afternoon, December 21st, my wife and I took Dolly to the veterinary hospital for a checkup, and it was determined that Dolly was to be kept overnight at the hospital. I was to pick her up the next day after she was given more fluids, assuming her condition improved. On Tuesday, December 22nd, the lead veterinarian, Dr. Stroud, discussed with us that Dolly's sudden onset diabetes with low electrolytes, which followed the previous diagnosis of Evan's Syndrome, was something that she and none of the other four veterinarians at the veterinary hospital could explain and had never even heard of before. In addition, none of the specialists and endocrinologists at a specialty veterinary hospital they collaborate with had any logical explanation for the reason Dolly acquired these two very serious, rare, and sudden onset lethal conditions. The prognosis looked bleak, but Dr. Stroud was hopeful because Dolly looked better, and her laboratory report was better after the treatment. Dr. Stroud offered to come in the next day, during her day off, and examine Dolly as well as provide another round of treatment to attempt to get her electrolytes and glucose levels normal. I left the veterinarian with hope that Dolly's condition would improve.

That night, after I brought my pugs their favorite rotisserie chicken dinner, my wife picked up her mother and brought her to our home. Just after my wife went to bed and while I was alone at the kitchen sink finishing cleaning up, her mother glided quickly out of her bedroom without her cane, which was not natural, since she was a very unsteady and slow walker, came up to me on the other side of the bar, and said with an evil grin, "Daisy is going to miss Dolly." I saw her grin first because she was looking down at the side of the bar and then she raised her gaze to meet mine and, in her eyes, I saw evil. I then asked her unemotionally and slowly, "Are you responsible for Dolly's illness?" She acted as though she was surprised that I would ask such a direct question, and all emotion left her face. After looking me directly into my eyes and saying nothing for three seconds, she slowly and unmistakably nodded her head two full times. I asked again with a louder voice to ensure that she clearly heard me. She continued to look at me with no emotion and total solemnity and nodded her head twice again. With evil in her eyes and a smiling expression (with no love nor sympathy in her eyes), she said "I will pray for her. My god listens to me." When my mother-in-law said "god", she meant her god, which is Satan. I was so shocked and outraged by what my mother-in-law said that I tried to tell my wife, but my wife, in typical fashion, reacted angrily, saying she did not believe me. As heart-wrenching as this was, it was not a total surprise to me.

I think it is reasonable to clarify that when I say my mother-in-law is possessed, that evaluation is coming from me directly, supported by the empirical evidence that I personally have witnessed, along with my perception of validation by God through the Holy Spirit. In fairness, no formal evaluation of her has been performed by medical personnel nor clergy. I certainly would not expect my mother-in-law to allow such an evaluation to happen. I also should clarify that before 2015, the demons possessing her seemed to be fairly weak and more of the mean-spirited, aspersion casting type, rather than the more dangerous type. That being said, I never trusted her and always locked my bedroom door when she was at my home. My wife acted like she never understood this, and she refused to believe me that I perceived her mother to be dangerous. However, during that visit in December of 2015, I perceived a much more powerful and much more evil presence in my mother-in-law. I hated having her in my home and in my life.

That night of December 22nd, after the awful encounter with my mother-in-law, Dolly had a horrible night. She periodically would wake up and have a difficult time breathing, and I moved her into our master bathroom, where she seemed to feel more comfortable. I stayed up with her all night, praying for her, and repeatedly blessing her with holy water. The next morning, Dolly looked much worse than the previous evening. However, before my wife and I were to drive her to the veterinarian, Dolly perked up and momentarily looked like her old, healthy self when I offered her a favorite treat. My wife and I decided to spare Dolly her usual daily pills, which she hated and needed to take the past few weeks, since we could see that this was going to be her last day. When Dr. Stroud saw Dolly's condition, she agreed that euthanasia was the merciful next step. I was completely devastated and heartbroken.

In the afternoon after the morning that Dolly was euthanized, my wife left the house to get her nails done. My mother-in-law was at her usual spot at our kitchen table. I decided to calmly confront her and have that confrontation both recorded on video with my compact digital camera and also record the audio with a popular app on my iPhone. Before I left my home office, I was careful to place the camera in movie mode, turned it on, and when I got to the kitchen, I placed it in an inconspicuous manner where she would not notice it, moments before I confronted her at the kitchen table. She did not look at it the entire time I was in the kitchen. While in my office, I also turned on the audio recording app on my iPhone and secured it in its holster. I sat down at the kitchen table across from my mother-in-law and asked her if she often perceives that I am not comfortable around her. She responded that she gets the impression I do not like her. I told my mother-in-law that I do not forgive the evil that the demon inside her has done to me and our family. I also reminded her of what she said to me about Dolly the night before. She calmly pretended not to know what I was speaking about. I calmly ended the discussion. I was still in shock, heartbroken, felt completely helpless regarding the entire situation, felt like I had no local human support, and did not want to execute any extreme actions that would have catastrophic consequences. After I collected my camera and got back to my office, I shut off both the camera and my iPhone app, and then got sidetracked with other items.

Late in the afternoon on Saturday, December 26th, I drove to Starbucks, and while stopped in the drive through line, I recalled the audio and video recordings that I had made of my mother-in-law. I listened to the iPhone audio recording app and noticed it cut off just after I had started the discussion with my mother-in-law. This was strange, since my iPhone was secure in its holster and should have required a manual operation to stop recording. I started thinking about the camera video and wondering whether or not it captured anything unusual. After returning from Starbucks, I was able to turn on the camera and watch the video, because there was more than sufficient battery charge. On the video, as soon as you see me step away from the camera to sit down, you see my mother-in-law at the table, and then the video cuts off.

One thing that I learned from this is that demons can come and go as they please, in terms of leaving a person that they have possessed and re-entering them at will. This would explain how my mother-in-law could go to church for years, even after she became possessed. The demons would simply leave her before she entered a church, and therefore, she would not manifest any of the dramatic symptoms sometimes seen when a possessed person enters a church.

I felt very low in energy by 7:30 PM that night. I tried to push myself to work out, but realized that I could not, and went to bed around 8 PM. Around 11 PM, I felt sick, on fire, and with an upset stomach. I prayed for healing and then slept until 8:30 AM, Sunday morning, but still felt queasy. I told my wife that I had felt sick the previous night as well as now, despite not drinking any alcohol nor eating anything unusual. I perceived the malaise was due to her mother. One of my sons was due to visit me via an airline and arrive the following day, but I was now worried about exposing him to my mother-in-law and her demons, because to me, she clearly had more "company" than before. In a soft and calm voice, I asked my wife to do me a favor and take her mother home today or early the next day. Otherwise, I planned to cancel my son's trip and not put him in harm's way. My wife angrily responded, but not at high volume, that her mother can stay as long as she wants and that she is also considering leaving me and taking my surviving pug DaisyMae with her. Close to 10 AM, I walked out of my office where I was having coffee to check on DaisyMae. I had just decided to tell my son to cancel the trip because of my mother-in-law's demons. To my surprise, my wife was loading her mother's things into her car. My wife said to me, "This is your lucky day. She wants to go home now. Don't say a word to me about it or I will leave with Daisy." It is interesting to note that my mother-in-law was in her usual guest bedroom on the other side of the house from my master bedroom, during the time I requested my wife to take her home. There is no way that she could have heard our conversation earlier that morning. I infer that the demons heard my earlier request to my wife and did not want the publicity for cancelling my son's visit. These unclean spirits prefer that their presence be hidden from humans. It had been a painful and costly visit by my mother-in-law. I lost my beloved Dolly, which my mother-in-law seemed to be very happy about.

I suspect that Dolly's condition worsened, and my malaise suddenly appeared because my mother-in-law had been welcomed into my home by my wife. I infer that a disembodied dark spirit is not as powerful as one that is within and controlling a malevolent human being, which has been willfully invited into the home of a victim. The attack on that victim is more ferocious and more difficult to defend against, especially if there is not someone trained regarding how to combat the evil. Before 2016, I was still in learning mode regarding how to combat evil. I had no mentoring, and relied on books, videos, and discussions with knowledgeable sources. I studied a lot more after what I went through in 2015 and became much better prepared.

I continued not feeling well and felt even worse while I attended church later that morning of Sunday, December 27th. I did penance and, per request, I also received healing and protection prayers from Father Vincenzo. I literally had been feeling my life energy being drained from me, as if from a psychic vampire, which is a very strange experience. During mass I had trouble concentrating and thought there may be a possibility that I could die. Therefore, after eucharist and prayer, while still in church, I texted important information to those people that care about me. I do not text in church, but this was a unique emergency, and I did not perceive that medical care could provide a cure. By the grace of God, I started feeling better, and I felt much better after I got home and reunited with my surviving pug, DaisyMae.

I am thankful to God for blessing me with my two pugs, Dolly Madison and DaisyMae, who brought me daily joy and love. I enjoyed many wonderful times with them, and they also helped me get through the difficult times. The following are two of my favorite photographs of them.

Dolly Madison and DaisyMae in 2010

On multiple occasions, regarding my mother-in-law, God has referred me to this Holy Scripture:

Beloved, never avenge yourselves, but
leave room for the wrath of God; for it is written,
'Vengeance is mine, I will repay, says the Lord.'

Romans: Chapter 12:19 (NRSV-CE)

On December 30th, God informed me that God's mission for me is to inform the good souls of this world about the reality of God and Satan as well as the dangers posed by Satan and his Forces of Evil before it is too late. God also wants me to promote large-scale collaboration and to organize and coordinate a response to this threat to humanity as well as provide guidance regarding how to address major problems that humanity is struggling with. No one has been highly visible and speaking publicly about the dangers posed by Satan, the prevalence of demons and the afflictions and tragedies that they cause daily, the impact of demons on nationwide social and political tensions, and the impact of demons on international political and military tensions.

God choosing me to share critical truths with humanity is a direct threat to Satan's current and future planned world order. Because of this, I recognized that I needed to do a large amount of preparation before going public. These preparations included not only continuing to learn more about spiritual warfare, but also enhancing security infrastructure, and preparing for potential physical combat, since Satan's human followers might become dangerous to me and others. In addition, I had read sources and seen credible interviews mentioning that there are some Satanists in the Catholic Church, just as it is reasonable to assume that there are a small percentage of Satanists in every large religion and in every profession. That is the reason I did not speak with anyone that I knew in the Catholic Church about the photograph before going public, because I did not want information about my experience to get to the wrong people and put myself at risk before I was ready.

So here are some of the thoughts that I had after I learned about God's plan for me:

1. I am the only human being that I know of in documented history, that has been threatened by Satan for offering to help mankind and has a visual artifact to prove it.

2. Until I go public, I will be harboring a secret that is vital to saving millions of lives, preventing nuclear war, and reducing a large amount of suffering. God must have planned this deception of Satan and my role a long time ago. I had lived my entire life up until 2015, without knowing about it. Now that I understand my mission, I feel like a secret agent working for God. If I would have been allowed to know my mission when I was much younger, I know that I would have lived a

very different life and studied additional subjects at the university and beyond. That being said, I realized that it is God's will that I lived the life that I did in order to have a more compelling testimony for humanity.

3. After I go public, I will need to be ever vigilant regarding the risks posed by the human contingent of the Forces of Evil. I have no desire for my life to resemble scenes from a fictional John Wick movie.

4. I need to come up with a strategy for presenting the new proof of God and Satan to the public in a manner that ensures credibility and maximum velocity for spreading the news, while preventing panic.

In 2019, there were additional, noteworthy acts of intimidation that I received directly from Satan, and they are unprecedented in their brashness and desperation.

- On May 29, 2019, at 1:15 AM, while my wife was asleep, and after I had just returned to bed after going to the bathroom, I heard two distinct low volume non-animal and non-human growling sounds coming through the baby monitor, which was next to my bed. I then heard Satan's angry voice state "That is what I am." Then he let loose with what to me was a very loud and chilling growl. My wife did not react, so I inferred that my hearing may have been a spiritual hearing. While it was scary, I immediately afterwards felt angry and unintimidated.

- On July 20, 2019, due to a tumor and bleeding condition that could not be remedied, my beloved pug, DaisyMae, had to be euthanized. She had lived to be 14 years old, two years longer than an average pug lifespan. In fact, in the Spring of 2017, she had been diagnosed with an auto-immune disorder, which was supposed to be terminal. However, each day I diligently prayed over her and she lived two more happy years. Nevertheless, on this day, I was very heartbroken. That evening, at just after 2 AM on July 21, 2019, while my wife was asleep, I had awakened to go to bathroom, but had not yet gotten up nor opened my eyes. I then distinctly heard Satan speaking to me through the baby monitor again saying "DaisyMae" five times at a low volume and mocking me cruelly. There is no limit to how evil Satan and demons are. Shortly thereafter, I experienced a splitting headache that got progressively worse. I took one 325mg aspirin and then another one fifteen minutes later. Three and a half hours later, the pain had not lessened. Realizing that additional medication was not an option, and more importantly, recognizing the source of the problem, I applied holy water, prayed, and the pain was completely gone within five minutes.

- For several years, I have been President of the HDI Central Florida Chapter. HDI is a professional association that provides globally recognized training and certifications for the Information Technology Service and Support community. I hold monthly calls with my local chapter officers. On August 13, 2019, I chaired one of these calls. I joined the conference line three minutes early and heard my fellow local chapter officer, James, who was the only other officer to join the call early. After we greeted one another, we then both heard a strange third male voice, who was also a very heavy breather. This intruder to the call was profane toward me and seemed to slow and slur his speech intentionally in order to disguise his voice. I told James that I would call him directly on his mobile telephone, and then I would conference in the two other local chapter officers. Just before I hung up on the conference line, the intruding caller said a couple of words in a non-slurred manner, and then I recognized that it was the same voice that threatened me through the baby monitor next to my bed. After I called James back and then conferenced in the two other local chapter officers, Sue and Joe, Joe said he had called in and only heard the music that you hear when no one else is on the conference line. Basically, he had called in after James and I disconnected from the conference line, so there was the usual music. It is important to note that I had been using FreeConference.com, and I always receive an e-mail summary report after each call that lists all telephone numbers that dialed into the conference call. That day, I received two separate e-mails: the first e-mail listed only my telephone number and James's telephone number. The key point is that the intruder's associated telephone number was not listed. The second e-mail was sent to me, because Joe and Sue called the conference line after James and I had already left. It listed Joe's and Sue's telephone numbers.

- On Friday, October 4th, I had a scheduled call with one of my HDI Chapter Sponsors. I used my same conference line from FreeConference.com because I did not know if my sponsor would ask anyone else to join. Seven minutes after Samantha and I started our call, an unexpected third person joined the call. A male, sounding professional, authoritative, and in his middle-40s joined the call and spoke as if he was speaking to multiple other people that were at the same place with him. I heard background murmuring as if there were multiple people with him. He did not identify himself until my second request. He then responded by saying his name is Michael Hawthorne. I asked Samantha if she invited anyone else to the call and she said no. I then asked Michael if he was with Samantha's company, and he responded with a very serious and somewhat menacing "Last week." In response to the obvious intruder, I told Samantha that I would call her back on her office telephone, and she agreed. As expected, I received an e-mail from FreeConference.com, but it only listed the telephone numbers for myself and Samantha. This marked the second conference call that included an intruder and a summary e-mail with no information about the intruder. On the morning of October 7th, I called FreeConference.com and spoke with Sarah from Customer Service. She informed me that I had been using an older, legacy platform, but that it was not possible for an unauthorized person to call into the conference line without my seeing their telephone number that they dialed in from on the subsequent e-mail report. She looked at my conference call record of October 4th and confirmed that she only saw a listing of my telephone number and Samantha's. I asked Sarah to have a high-level technical manager call me to discuss the unusual events. That afternoon, Operations Manager Will Reed called me back. Will emphasized that it is impossible for any unauthorized person to join my conference line and not have their telephone number show up on the report that is e-mailed to me. He said that, in the distant past, he had heard of someone dialing in with a mobile telephone and people on the conference call could hear the mobile telephone unintentionally picking up another mobile call in the background, but that there was no interactions possible with that external party. When I told Will that the intruder on my two conference calls could interact with everyone on the conference line, and that the intruder's telephone number did not show up on the e-mail reports, he shouted in great surprise, "What?!" That is all that I needed to know, and I was not surprised. Spiritual beings are pure energy and both inhuman and human spirits seem to have an easy time interacting with electricity and electronic equipment.

CHAPTER 8: THE IMMORTALITY OF THE SOUL

Before we can obtain a detailed understanding of the purpose of life and how demons can affect human beings, we need to understand the immortality of the soul.

One of the challenges of being a human being is figuring out what is really going on. What is the scope of reality, what are the rules to live by, and what are we striving to achieve? When you are born, you typically obtain everything necessary for life from your parents. Hopefully, as you are raised, you receive teachings from them about the realities of life, rules and laws that must be followed, ideals, values, the importance of virtues, the meaning of the Holy Scriptures, and the importance of a good relationship with God. Unfortunately, too often in our modern world, children are raised without a sense of life's purpose, with no foundation in faith and spiritual matters, and no teachings regarding the dangers of this world, both natural and supernatural. Most of us would like to have helpful instruction manuals when it comes to assembling anything with many parts, video games, and anything else that is complex. Why are we not presented with a helpful instruction manual for how to be successful in life? The Holy Scriptures are only helpful for those that study them. Recent surveys have shown a dramatic decline in the number of people that consider themselves affiliated with a specific religion. Our world is more dangerous than it has ever been, due to this decline in religious practices, the ubiquitous availability of the internet, fake news, harmful content, the increasing prevalence of human predators, the rise in hate groups, and the rising military and economic ambitions of people that are easily manipulated by the Forces of Evil.

Each human being is born into a world at war and there are only two sides: 1) the Forces of Good serving the God of all creation, and 2) the Forces of Evil serving Satan. It is every human being's responsibility to choose a side and to exemplify that choice through actions. God loves us as human beings and therefore enables each human being to exercise free will.

As Dr. M. Scott Peck, M.D. mentioned in his book, *Glimpses of the Devil,* which is subtitled, *A Psychiatrist's Personal Accounts of Possession, Exorcism, and Redemption* (Peck, 2005), there are two states of being: submission to God or enslavement to the Forces of Evil. Famous author and theologian, C.S. Lewis, explained in "Christianity and Culture", contained in *Christian Reflections* (Hooper ed., 1967) that "There is no neutral ground in the universe: every square inch, every split second is claimed by God and counterclaimed   by   Satan."

Virtually every human being wonders what this thing called life is all about. Each one of us is born into this world for the purpose of helping others and through continuous development, learning, and good works, our mission should be to enhance our soul by being the best that we can be. Every religion has sacred writings and or oral traditions that describe this in a detailed manner.

This paragraph is a short course in advanced human anatomy. The essential you is a spiritual being called a soul and it is immortal. Your soul is comprised of your mind, will, and emotions. In other words, your personality is part of your soul. During a lifetime, your soul lives inside a body. I like to think of the following metaphor. God created each human being like a two-seat sports car, where your body is the sports car body, your soul is supposed to be in the driver seat, and the passenger seat is supposed to be filled with the Holy Spirit. If you do not fill the passenger seat with the Holy Spirit, then there is a risk that something else can get into that seat and cause distractions and problems for you.

I have personally experienced many interactions with disembodied spirits, both human and inhuman. I also have spoken to many people who have had paranormal experiences. Sometimes, they are inspired to share stories with me even though I did not ask about their experiences. During a social visit, I was surprised to hear from the mother of a friend of my son, that she used to be tormented by a dark spirit called a shadow person, which on several nights would sit on her bed and touch her hair, while she pretended to be asleep, frozen in terror. I have also spoken to people, including those close to me, who have seen recently deceased loved ones, sometimes on multiple occasions. Another time, I recall preparing to get off an airline flight, when the passenger in front of me started talking to me. She said she worked at a hospice. I responded saying that it takes a very special and caring type of person to work at a hospice. She agreed and went on to say that she has seen both very beautiful things and very scary things. I immediately received a rapid and condensed feed of paranormal visualizations that coincided with her comment.

You would be surprised how many people, including people that you know, have had paranormal experiences, but choose not to openly discuss them, because they are worried about being ridiculed or thinking about it causes them to be uncomfortable. Despite the increasing popularity of paranormal-themed television series, movies, and YouTube videos, a significant portion of which are questionable in terms of authenticity, many people are hesitant to admit that they have had paranormal experiences. Nevertheless, understanding that your soul is immortal is extremely important. How you choose to live your life affects not only the quality of your current life, but your future as well. In terms of proof of the immortality of the soul, it might surprise you that there is a significant amount of research and books published, and much of this research has been conducted by medical doctors.

Dr. Raymond A. Moody, Jr. coined the term Near-Death Experience (NDE), and in his book, *Life After Life* (Moody Jr., 1975), he analyzed the common out of body experiences of over one hundred patients. Despite the wide variety of patient backgrounds, cultures, beliefs, and medical situations, during an NDE, each patient experienced an overwhelming feeling of peace and well-being, including freedom from pain; the impression of being located outside one's physical body; floating or drifting through darkness, sometimes described as a tunnel; becoming aware of a golden light; encountering deceased loved ones and or a "being of light"; having a rapid succession of visual images of one's past; and experiencing another world of much beauty. Dr. Moody inspired on-going and extensive studies of the NDE phenomenon.

In her book, *On Life After Death* (Kübler-Ross, 1991), Dr. Elisabeth Kübler-Ross mentioned that similar experiences of NDE were had by over 20,000 patients. She shared in her own compelling personal experiences, including an impactful visitation by a Mrs. Schwarz, who had died months before. She also described the astounding experiences of specific patients. During an NDE, each patient was free of physical handicaps, and had full perception of all the activity that was going on around them, despite vital signs being absent. A patient who had been blind many years was able to describe accurate visual details. One patient told her father that she was met by her brother, even though she did not have any living siblings, and had never been told that her parents had a son who died three months before she was born.

Interesting research has been conducted at the University of Virginia School of Medicine Division of Perceptual Studies (DOPS). As described on their website (https://med.virginia.edu/perceptual-studies/), the Division's main purpose, and the *raison d'être* for its foundation, is the scientific empirical investigation of phenomena that suggest that currently accepted scientific assumptions and theories about the nature of mind and consciousness, and relationships to physical matter, may be incomplete. Examples of such phenomena, sometimes called *paranormal*, include various types of extrasensory perception (such as telepathy), apparitions and deathbed visions (sometimes referred to as after-death communications or

ADCs), poltergeists, experiences of persons who come close to death and survive (usually called near-death experiences or NDEs), out-of-body experiences (OBEs), and claimed memories of previous lives.

DOPS is a unit of the Psychiatry and Neurobehavorial Sciences of the University of Virginia's Health System. It was founded in 1967, when Dr. Ian Stevenson resigned as Chairman of the Department of Psychiatry to become Director of the Division and Chester F. Carlson Professor of Psychiatry, positions he served in for the next 35 years. The Division was made possible initially through the endowment of an Eminent Scholars Chair to which Dr. Stevenson was appointed. The Division's principal benefactor was the late Chester F. Carlson, the inventor of xerography, gave the first and largest contribution of funds for the endowed professorship. At his death in 1968, Mr. Carlson also left the University a bequest for the support of the Division's work. Early in 2002, Dr. Bruce Greyson, who has been a faculty member at DOPS since 1995, formerly the long-time editor of the *Journal of Near-Death Studies*, took over as director and Carlson Professor of Psychiatry. This allowed Dr. Stevenson to devote more time to writing books and articles about his research into cases of the reincarnation type. In September of 2014, Dr. Bruce Greyson retired from the directorship and Dr. Jim Tucker, Bonner-Lowry Associate Professor of Psychiatry and Neurobehavioral Sciences, became the Director of the Division of Perceptual Studies. Dr. Tucker has authored two books thus far on his research into the phenomena of children who claim to remember previous lives. His most recent book *Return to Life: Extraordinary cases of Children Who Remember Past Lives* was published in 2013, and his first book *Life Before Life: A Scientific Investigation of Children's Memories of Previous Lives* was published in 2005.

I believe that you will find their books as well as internet-posted videos on their research with children reporting past lives to be very compelling. Additional research can be found in Dr. Brian Weiss's book, *Many Lives, Many Masters* (Weiss, 1988), which documents his experience delivering psychiatric cures for modern conditions through past-life therapy. A graduate of Columbia University and Yale Medical School, Brian L. Weiss M.D. is Chairman Emeritus of Psychiatry at the Mount Sinai Medical Center in Miami. According to his website (https://www.brianweiss.com/), "as a traditional psychotherapist, Dr. Brian Weiss was astonished and skeptical when one of his patients began recalling past-life traumas that seemed to hold the key to her recurring nightmares and anxiety attacks. His skepticism was eroded, however, when she began to channel messages from "the space between lives," which contained remarkable revelations about Dr. Weiss's family and his dead son. Using past-life therapy, he was able to cure the patient and embark on a new, more meaningful phase of his own career."

Near death experiences have been widely written about and there are many books, internet videos, and movies that cover true experiences. Highly acclaimed examples include:

- Dr. Raymond A. Moody, Jr.'s book, *Life After Life*, published by HarperSanFrancisco (Moody Jr., 1975)

- Dr. Elisabeth Kübler-Ross's book, *On Life After Death*, Published by Celestial Arts (Kübler-Ross, 1991)

- Dr. Eben Alexander III's book, *Proof of Heaven: A Neurosurgeon's Journey into the Afterlife*, published by Simon & Schuster Paperbacks (Alexander III, 2012)

- Todd Burpo and Lynn Vincent co-wrote *Heaven is for Real: A Little Boy's Astounding Story of His Trip to Heaven and Back*, published by Thomas Nelson. This book was the basis for the movie, *Heaven Is For Real* (Burpo and Vincent, 2014).

If all the above are not compelling enough with regard to the immortality of the soul, consider the following case involving the miraculous rescue of baby Lily Groesbeck from the Spanish Fork River in Utah on the morning of March 7, 2015. According to an article on www.lifedaily.com entitled, "Questions Arise After Cops Hear Strange Voice Call Out For Help At Car Crash Site",

The night of March 6, Jennifer Lynn Groesbeck, 25, was driving home to Springville from Salem, where she had been visiting her father. At around 10:30 p.m. her car must have gone off the road where Arrowhead Trail connects with Main Street. Because of where the vehicle landed, it was difficult for anyone to see the wreck from the street above. Then, about 14 hours later, on Saturday at 12:30 p.m., a fisherman spotted the overturned vehicle and called the police. Spanish Fork

Police Officer Bryan Dewitt was one of the first officers to arrive. The incident was originally reported as a possible abandoned vehicle in the river, but as he got closer, he could see the mother inside. Three more officers arrived almost simultaneously at the river and that's when they heard a voice. "We were down on the car and a distinct voice said, 'Help me, help me.'" Another officer, Tyler Beddoes, said that this voice wasn't something that was just in our heads. "It was as plain as day," he said. Officer Beddoes even recalls Officer Dewitt saying, "'We're trying…We're trying our best to get in there.'" But he didn't know how to explain it. Still, the mysterious voice which sounded like a woman and not a child pushed every officer to get into that overturned car. None of them intended on flipping a car over that day, but they knew there was someone that needed help. When the officers jumped into the 10-ft-deep river and flipped the Dodge sedan onto its side, they discovered no one inside was able to speak. The only people in the car were a deceased mother and an infant. "I was terrified there was a little baby," Dewitt said. "My initial instinct was that she was dead." The little girl was hanging upside down, but her head was not touching the water. The responders initially did not see her, but when they got the car turned over, they spotted her and raced to get her out. After Dewitt discovered the child, firefighters Paul Taultomadakis and Lee Mecham jumped on top of the vehicle. They got the door open and Mecham jumped up and held the door while Dewitt got down inside, grabbed the baby girl, and…lifted her out of the car seat. The officers didn't think about anything except trying to save the child and they were able to cut her out of the car. After Officer Taultomadakis pulled the toddler named Lily out, they started passing her around until she got into Officer Jared Warner's arms. The first thing he noticed was Lily's eyes fluttering. It was a positive sign of life for everyone, but they knew Lily wasn't out of harm's way. Warner then ran up the hill with her and into an ambulance and they drove off. He started CPR and did anything he could just to save her. The officers still remaining at the scene had just spent 20 minutes in the frigid waters, and being so focused on the rescue, they didn't realize the impact it was having on their bodies. Officer Beddoes, who stood at 6 ft tall had the water level at his neck and said he didn't feel the cold because he wasn't paying attention to himself. But after several minutes he started to feel the effects. The four officers and three firefighters were then brought to the hospital to be treated for hypothermia. The unconscious 18-month-old regained her consciousness at the intensive care unit at Primary Children's Hospital. When her grandfather and aunt and uncle arrived, they believed that she would spend weeks in the ICU alone. If Lily recovered at all, doctors warned the family that she could face brain damage, paralysis, or other long-term effects as a result of the 14 hours she spent suspended upside down in her car seat in the frigid SUV. Instead, after five days, Lily was blowing kisses, singing nursery rhymes and insisting on being held by her favorite grandfather. But questions still remain for Baby Lily. After being released from the hospital, Lily's uncle, Garrett

Groesbeck was given temporary custody of her, but permanent custody was to be decided later on. After a toxicology report, authorities confirmed that Jennifer had drugs in her system when the vehicle struck a barrier at the bridge. The medical examiner found a mixture of Clonazepam, THC, morphine, codeine, and hydromorphone in the deceased mother's system. The report also indicated the presence of 6-monoacetylmorphine-free, which is indicative of heroin use. Jennifer died "as a result of blunt force injury of the head."

The men who found the SUV overturned in that cold river on March 7 have since met with the Groesbeck family and told them about the mysterious voice they heard crying for help inside the car, leading them to a rapid rescue. "What this should show all of us is an acknowledgement of how Jenny loved her little girl," Lily's uncle, Garrett Groesbeck said. "I don't think there can be any stronger example of loving someone so much, even after death. The fact that we have these men, not just one person, but all of these men that had the same experience, really hit home with us," he continued. The family, members of The Church of Jesus Christ of Latter-day Saints believe that Lily was truly protected by a higher power.

A video of a CNN interview with rescue personnel is here: https://www.youtube.com/watch?v=tTqLp_iYpxs&feature=emb_logo

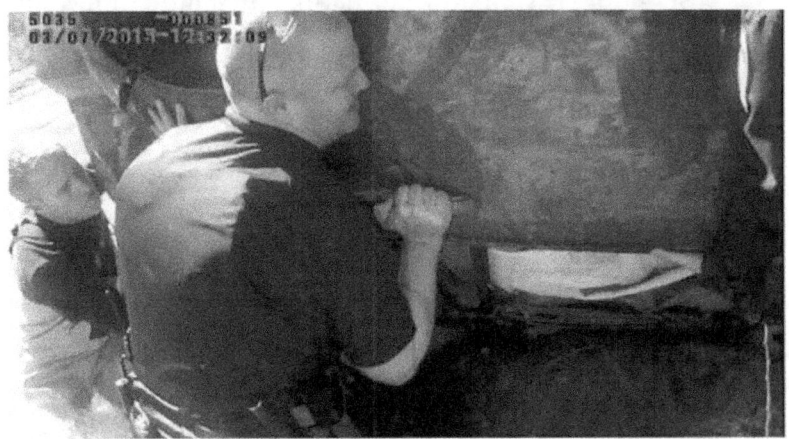

CHAPTER 9: HOW DEMONS AFFECT HUMAN BEINGS

Now that we understand the immortality of the soul, we can obtain a better understanding of what Satan and his demons are attempting to accomplish. Ever since Lucifer betrayed God, was renamed Satan, and was cast out of Heaven down to Earth with a third of the angels, all of them being demons, they have inflicted their revenge upon humanity. The goals for Satan and his Forces of Evil are this: to destroy as much of humanity as possible and take as many souls hostage as possible. Their secondary goals are to cause chaos, ruin relationships, reduce quality of life, and to destroy human happiness.

The demons' strategy for human manipulation, destruction, and world domination is primarily based upon deception. The most prevalent deception that Satan plagues the world with is the lie that there is no God, no Satan, and no spiritual world. If a human being does not believe in God nor Satan, they will not pursue a relationship with God, will not actively practice a God-centric religion, and will not do behaviors that provide protection against evil. In addition, if they are unaware of how demons can affect human beings, then they are completely vulnerable to demonic attack and demonic manipulation.

Satan's deception of humanity is so widespread, persistent, and ancient, that many people throughout history have written and spoken about it. Below are a few relevant quotes:

- John Wilkinson, in his book *Quakerism Examined (Wilkinson, 1836)*, wrote: "One of the artifices of Satan is to induce men to believe that he does not exist; another, perhaps equally fatal, is to make them fancy that he is obliged to stand quietly by, and not to meddle with them, if they get into true silence."

- In *Spiritualism, a Satanic Delusion, and a Sign of the Times (Ramsey, 1856)*, Pastor William Ramsey included this passage: "One of the most striking proofs of the personal existence of Satan, which our times afford us, is found in the fact that he has so influenced the minds of multitudes in reference to his existence and doings, as to make them believe that he does not exist; and that the hosts of Demons or Evil Spirits, over whom Satan presides as Prince, are only the fantasies of the brain, some hallucination of mind. Could we have a stronger proof of the existence of a mind so mighty as to produce such results?"

- Charles Pierre Baudelaire, a nineteenth century poet, essayist, and translator, wrote in the Paris newspaper "Le Figaro", in 1864, "The Devil's cleverest wile is to make men believe that he does not exist."

- C.S. Lewis, in *The Weight of Glory* (Lewis, 1941), wrote: "Like a good chess player, Satan is always trying to maneuver you into a position where you can save your castle only by losing your bishop."

- T.D. Jakes, Bishop of The Potter's House, a non-denominational American megachurch, stated: "You are not going to defeat this devil with will power — you need the power of God, and if you lose your faith, you've lost the fight."

- Bishop Fulton J. Sheen: "Very few people believe in the devil these days, which suits the devil very well. He is always helping to circulate the news of his own death. The essence of God is existence, and He defines Himself as: 'I am Who am.' The essence of the devil is the lie, and he defines himself as: 'I am who am not.' Satan has very little trouble with those who do not believe in him; they are already on his side."

The greatest danger to human beings, causing everything from unnecessary individual arguments and conflicts, irrational racism and xenophobia, hate-driven organized terrorism, and war, is due to deliberate demonic manipulation. That is not to say that every human interaction or argument is affected by demons. However, when human beings do not understand how demons work, it enables demons to plant negative, harmful, and destructive thoughts in their minds, "push their buttons", and cause unnecessary conflict. For example, if person number one is given a negative impression about a person number two, and person number two attempts to communicate with person number one, person number one will not hear nor comprehend person number two in the same way that an open-minded person would hear and comprehend person number two. It does not matter where the negative impression comes from, whether based upon legitimate reasons and previous actions of person number two or whether the negative impressions have been artificially planted in person number one by a demon. The result will be the same, whereby person number one will be less receptive to person number two, and there probably will be a miscommunication leading to a negative interaction. If a demon can create a negative mindset between two people, it makes it a lot easier to perpetuate the negativity and cause continuous and escalating conflicts. This situation occurs in places of employment, in marriages, and in other personal relationships.

Even though demons do not obtain sustenance from food like human beings, they do need to feed off of negative emotional energies, including those associated with the seven deadly sins (also called cardinal sins) committed by human beings: pride (or vanity), envy, gluttony, greed, lust, sloth, and anger (or wrath). During exorcism, some demons will even claim that their names match the names of these sins. Demons derive the most energy from human anger and fear, which is why the most common actions of demons are to create conflict and anger between human beings and to create human fear either by fear-inspiring human behaviors or through direct preternatural activity.

In the case of preternatural activity, such as in demonic infestation of a home, it is a terrifying experience for the people that live there, because the demonic intimidation always escalates. If the people do not engage the assistance of clergy to drive away the demonic presence, very bad things will happen. Examples of demonic infestation preternatural activity can include shocking scratching noises inside walls, loud noises in the middle of the night, objects disappearing, objects being thrown violently seemingly by themselves, furniture being moved around, physical injuries such as scratches appearing on occupants, and occupants suffering from profound weakness and lack of energy, sickness, and even death. Usually, after an experienced member of the clergy is engaged to bless or "cleanse" the home of the evil presence, there is an immediate positive change to the environment and the preternatural activity ceases. In more difficult cases, it may take more than one clergy visit. Simply relocating without engaging clergy is not advised, since the demonic presence might simply follow the people to the next residence. It is also possible that the demonic presence is due to the actions of one of the occupants. That is why analysis and discernment are very important to understanding the root cause of the problem. Once this root cause is known, it is easier to solve the problem.

Saint Augustine claimed that, if God allowed Satan to have complete freedom to do as he would prefer, "no man would be left alive." Since demons desire to take as many lives as possible, they work closely together to orchestrate mass casualty events such as mass shootings, terrorism, and war. Most people without faith will view these as unrelated and even the frequency of mass shooting events to be coincidence as opposed to a deliberate campaign of evil against humanity. Demons have several advantages against human beings: they can communicate instantly worldwide via telepathy and do not need smartphones for texting and e-mail, they do not need sleep nor food and can be relentless in their attacks, they naturally collaborate with other demons, and they are never confused regarding their goals due to a micro-managing despot in Satan.

As mentioned earlier, social isolation is a typical approach that a demon uses to weaken a targeted human being. Just as in standard military warfare, one army will often attempt to cut off supply lines of fuel, ammunition, food, and water to the enemy. In analogous fashion, a demon will attempt to cut off human supply lines of emotional support and inter-personal communications.

There are three levels of demonic attack, which follow a progression in this order: 1) demonic oppression (sometimes called affliction), 2) demonic obsession (sometimes called attachment), and 3) demonic possession.

During demonic oppression, the demon will afflict a person by concurrently attempting to create rifts in personal relationships, sour their employer's view of them to the point of causing termination, cause financial hardship, cause physical ailments, and other difficulties. An oppressed and isolated human being that is not strong in faith will typically become depressed, feel sorry for themselves, and will often suffer from low self-esteem. Unless the situation is remediated, it will get worse.

During demonic obsession, the demon attacks a person's mind and will torment the person with repetitive negative thoughts to pummel self-esteem and to coerce destructive behavior. This has major implications for causality of suicide, where a demon will convince the targeted human being of the lies that no one loves them, there is nobody available to help them, and that tomorrow will not be better than today. When it comes to a demonic attempt to cause suicide, a demon or demons will not only afflict the victim, but they often will manipulate the behavior of influential people in the victim's life, such as to inspire them to behave in a hateful manner and possibly send hateful texts and social media posts. Suicide is a leading cause of death, and disproportionately, young people and Veterans are victims. We can do a better job of preventing suicide. A subsequent chapter will cover this topic in more detail.

Demonic obsession also has a major impact for causality of alcoholism, the opioid epidemic, other substance abuse, and deleterious behavioral addictions. Having a demon or demons relentlessly remind a victim of their physiological and mental craving for a harmful substance that they are addicted to, makes it much harder for the victim to break the habit. Proper psychiatric care, medication, and a support group are often required, but if natural evidence-based protocols are not effective, they should be supplemented with healthy spiritual practices and deliverance. A subsequent chapter will cover this topic in more detail.

The third level of demonic attack is possession. Possession is a condition when a demon or multiple demons have control over a person's body. The Catholic Church has a strict vetting process, whereby anyone that requests an exorcism must first have a thorough physical exam as well as a psychiatric evaluation to ensure that the person's symptoms are not caused by a natural medical condition. The Catholic Church also has four criteria for confirming that a human being is afflicted with demonic possession: aversion to the sacred, knowledge of a language or languages that the person has not studied, knowledge of the unknown, and physical strength far beyond what a typical human being of comparable age and stature should have. In terms of aversion to the sacred, a possessed person may be unable to walk into a house of worship, be unable to pray, act like holy water burns them, and act sickened or repulsed by sacred objects. Often, a possessed person will be able to speak fluently in a foreign language that they have never studied. They often can speak in Latin and other ancient languages because it is the demon that is speaking. Knowledge of the unknown means that the possessed person will say things that they could not possibly know. They may comment about a sin that you did in your past or something you did this morning that no other human being on Earth would know. Another sign of demonic possession is supernatural strength. One exorcist recounted to me that during an exorcism, a small teenage girl lifted a two-hundred-and-fifty-pound man up off the floor and threw him across the room.

In most cases for an unwilling possessed victim, the soul will have control of its body most of the time, but the demons are often sufficiently disruptive as to prevent the person from living a happy life. In many cases, due to the demon's behavior, which often includes antisocial behavior and outbursts of profanity and violence, the person will lose their job, damage important relationships, and cause destruction.

For unwilling victims of possession, the incidence is relatively rare compared to other levels of demonic attack. I have heard several Catholic exorcists in the United States estimate that of all the people referred to them for an exorcism in any given year, only one to three percent are genuine cases of possession. On the other hand, in Italy, there are exorcists today who perform a much larger number of exorcisms, and the percentage of people asking for exorcism and considered genuinely possessed, is much higher. As noted in THE TABLET in February of 2018, https://www.thetablet.co.uk/news/8622/number-of-exorcisms-in-italy-triples-, "The number of exorcisms in Italy has tripled recently, with experts predicting that around 500,000 requests are made a year." Father Paolo Carlin, a Capuchin Friar and spokesman for the International Association for Exorcists told Italian newspaper Corriere della Sera "All the people who come to us suffer, but they are many and we are few." Father Cesare Truqui, who was trained by Father Gabriel Amorth, told Vatican News "Many Christians no longer believe in the existence [of evil]. Few exorcists are appointed and there are no more young priests willing to learn the doctrine and practice of liberation of souls."

In fact, the demand is so high in parts of Italy, that a relatively recent practice of deliverance service is being held for the purpose of conducting spiritual deliverance for many people at the same time. Entire facilities have even been constructed for this purpose. There are also a significant number of exorcists that are conducting exorcisms remotely, either by smartphone or by web conferencing, because the demand for deliverance is high and increasing, and many people are unable to travel long distances nor incur the expenses of traveling to meet with an exorcist in person.

The shortage of exorcists and the lack of availability of exorcisms continues to be a problem. Due to concerns about the risk of potential law suits as well as a lack of belief in Satan among the clergy, especially at the level of bishop and above, there are many locations and even entire nations where it is not possible to obtain an exorcism delivered by local resources. The same is true for non-Christian religions. In addition, for those clergy that do believe, there is a shortage of proper training, and the increasing demand for spiritual deliverance compounds the problem.

There is no specific demographic for determining who is most likely to become possessed. Victims represent every type of categorization, including nationality, race, socio-economic status, level of education, religious or non-religious, etc. There are many ways that an unwilling victim can become possessed. There are documented cases when the victim had been dedicated to Satan while in utero or as a child by evil parents, often during a Satanic ritual. Sometimes, the victim has been the target of a curse, hex, or evil eye. Other times, the entry point for the demonic has been through the victim's practicing of the occult, such as with an Ouija board, tarot cards, scrying mirror, crystal ball, conducting astral projection or performing witchcraft. Seeking out mediums, palm readers, and fortune tellers can also expose a person to a demonic entry point. There are also many cases of untrained professionals and thrill seekers going ghost hunting in cemeteries and locations known to have paranormal activity. Anyone that participates in these activities attracts the attention of the spirit world and can expose a person to the attention of human or inhuman spirits, which can disrupt their life. For any unwilling victim that becomes possessed, exorcism and practicing a healthy spiritual lifestyle is required for liberation from evil demons.

A completely different type of possession is called perfect possession, which is when a human being willfully welcomes and accepts demonic possession in return for power, fame, wealth, success, and or any other perceived benefit. The famous priest and prolific author, Father Malachi Martin, said, "If you meet someone who is perfectly possessed, run." People that are perfectly possessed often appear like normal people. They may be government officials, physicians, attorneys, educators, stockbrokers, and other respected members of an organization or community. They may even be someone that you have worked with for years. There is an old expression, "the eyes are the windows to the soul." For these perfectly possessed people, there comes a time when you look into their eyes, and even though it may be someone that you have worked with or known for years, suddenly you realize that you are looking into the eyes of a different personality. It is typically a short-lived experience, unless the person has an uncharacteristic venting of anger or temper tantrum. That is how you might recognize this phenomenon. Completely uncharacteristic behaviors may be another indication. Perfectly possessed people typically do not seek nor desire exorcism, because they have willfully accepted their condition in exchange for some perceived advantage or reward.

An unusual situation that I have witnessed is what I call demonic symbiosis. Demons have a difficult existence outside of a human body, presumably being abused and tormented by more powerful demons that disparage and punish them for not being productive harming human beings. A demon prefers to reside in a human being for multiple reasons: the demon can experience human senses to their delight, they avoid persecution by other more powerful demons, and they can also cause physical harm, murder, and mayhem. While the person possessed by a demon in this situation may have originally become possessed against their will or without their knowledge because of a curse or other cause, the person may not realize that they are possessed, unless their life is significantly disrupted or if they have a lot of periods of time that they cannot remember. In some cases, a soul will not have a memory of what happens when a demon pushes them aside and takes over their body. This happens in some exorcisms, when the person goes into a trance, and the demon takes over until the demon is expelled or the exorcism is over. Afterwards, the person has no recollection of anything they did nor anything that happened during the ritual. In the case of demonic symbiosis, if the person does not experience destructive behaviors and experiences that are due to their demon, then they will go on living life without perceiving the need for spiritual deliverance. The same is true for someone who eventually becomes aware of their demonic possession but perceives an advantage or reward that comes with their condition. This type of person will not seek an exorcism. I have seen this and infer that many of the weaker demons are satisfied to cohabitate with a human being in secret and prefer to go unnoticed. The indications that a person is possessed with demonic symbiosis may arise from their presentation of a completely different personality, a different entity's voice, or radically uncharacteristic behaviors. These occurrences will typically be sporadic and infrequent because the weaker demons desire to stay hidden, so that anyone witnessing an anomaly will most likely disregard it. The more powerful and malevolent demons occur in the cases of perfect possession and possession of unwilling victims, and they utilize possession for much more harmful and destructive ends.

In *An Exorcist Tells His Story*, (Amorth, 1999), Father Gabriele Amorth describes how a human being can become a target of extraordinary demonic activity:

"1. *With God's permission.* I want to make absolutely clear that nothing happens without God's permission. It is also absolutely clear that God does not wish evil for anyone, but he allows it when it is our will (since he created us with completely free will), and he can use everything, even evil, for our own good. The characteristic of the first category of extraordinary demonic activity is complete absence of human guilt; it is entirely due to a diabolical intervention. God always allows normal satanic activity — temptation — and gives us all the graces necessary to resist, with the resulting good of strengthening our spiritual life. In the same manner, God at times also allows extraordinary satanic activity — possession, evil influences — to increase our humility, patience, and mortification. We have already given a couple of examples of this category: an external action of the devil that causes physical pain (such as the beatings and floggings suffered by the Cure of Ars and Padre Pio) or when a so-called oppression is allowed, as we have mentioned concerning Job and Saint Paul. The lives of many saints include examples of this affliction. Among modern saints, I can cite two who have been beatified by Pope John Paul II: Father Giovanni Calabria and Sister Mary of Jesus Crucified (who was the first Arab to be beatified). In both cases, and without any human fault, they were subjected to periods of true satanic possession. During those periods, the two saints did and said things totally incompatible with their holiness without the least fault, because it was the devil who acted through their bodies.

2. *When we are subjected to an evil spell.* This is another case in which the victim is completely blameless. Here, however, there is some human activity, but it is performed by those who cast the spell or those who hire a witch to cast it…. Here I will simply say that an evil spell *is causing the suffering of others through the intervention of the devil.* This intervention can take many different forms: binding, the evil eye, a curse. I will say right away that the most common method is sorcery.

3. *A grave and hardened state of sin.* Here we are addressing the cause that today,

unfortunately, is on the increase, with a resulting increase in the numbers of people who are victims of the devil. At the root, *the true cause is always a lack of faith.* As lack of faith increases, so does superstition; it is almost a mathematical reality….

4. *Association with evil people and places.* This category includes the practice or assisting in the practice of seances, witchcraft, satanic cults, or sects — which culminate in black masses — the occult...associating with warlocks, witch doctors, or certain types of card readers. These are all activities that make us vulnerable to evil spells. If we go so far as to desire a relationship with Satan, there is such a thing as consecration to Satan, the blood pact with Satan, attendance at satanic schools, and the election to the priesthood of Satan. Unfortunately, in the past fifteen years, we have witnessed an increase, almost an explosion, of these types of associations.

A very common example of associating with warlocks or witch doctors is this: Someone who is the victim of a stubborn illness cannot find any remedy. Someone else experiences all sorts of misfortune and believes that it is due to an evil influence. They appeal to a card reader or a warlock, who tells them, "You are subject to an evil spell." Up to now, there is very little damage done. However, unfortunately what follows is something like this: "For one thousand dollars — or more — I will cure you." These fees can be as high as $35,000. If the individual agrees, the card reader or warlock asks for some personal item: a photograph, a piece of underwear, a lock of hair, a few hairs, or a nail clipping. At this point, the evil act is accomplished. What does the warlock do with these items? He obviously uses them to practice black magic.

Unfortunately, many fall victim to these individuals because these sorcerers are often women who are always seen in church, or because the room of the warlock is blanketed with crucifixes, portraits of saints, the Blessed Virgin, and portraits of Padre Pio. The victims are also often told, "I practice only white magic; if you asked me for black magic I would refuse." In current terminology, white magic means to take away a spell; black magic means to cast a spell. In reality, as Father Candido never ceased to repeat, there are no such things as "white" and "black" magic; there is only black magic. Every form of magic is practiced with recourse to Satan. Therefore, the poor victim who went to the warlock with a minor evil influence (or probably without any such influence) goes home with a true, full-blown one. When this occurs, often we exorcists have to work much harder after the ill-fated action of the warlocks than we would have if the person had come to us with the original complaint."

During a presentation in January of 2020 at a retreat entitled, The Necessity of Exorcists, Father Vincent Lampert said that there are eight ways that a human being can open the door to demonic engagement:

1. Participating in occult practices

2. Ritual dedication to a demon, such as parents dedicating a child to a demon

3. Inviting a demon in

4. Being targeted by a curse (or casting a curse on someone else per #1)

5. Leading a life of habitual sin

6. Use of pornography

7. Broken relationships leading to unhealed emotional wounds, persistent feelings of hurt, resentment, and anger

8. Entertainment, such as books, movies, video games, card games, etc., that lead to unhealthy isolation and or occult practices

Clearly, the safest way to live is to abstain from behaviors that produce vulnerabilities, create addictions, and attract the attention of the Forces of Evil. That being said, many people suffer by the deliberate evil actions of others. Before I performed research on this matter, I had no idea how prevalent witchcraft is in the United States and around the world. You can do a search with your internet search engine of choice and find countless witch covens, and there is probably at least one based not far from where you live. If you go into one of the large retail chain bookstores, you will typically see a few shelves filled with bibles and associated reference books; but you will see vastly more shelves and even entire racks of books dedicated to various forms of witchcraft. Here in 2020, you do not even need to visit a physical bookstore. A simple internet search yields countless books about practicing witchcraft and Satanism that you can order online as well as electronic books that you can download. On a hunch, I conducted a search of smartphone apps available for download, and I was able to find multiple apps for practicing witchcraft, each including a substantial quantity of spells organized by category.

Surveys over the last few decades have shown that witchcraft, sometimes called Wicca, is one of the fastest growing religions in the United States. According to a Newsweek article, "Number Of Witches Rises Dramatically Across U.S. As Millennials Reject Christianity", by Benjamin Fearnow, dated November 18, 2018:

- The number of witches and Americans practicing Wicca religious rituals increased dramatically since the 1990s, with several recent studies indicating there may be at least 1.5 million witches across the country, which is more followers than the 1.4 million mainline members of the Presbyterian church.

- The increase has been led by a rejection of mainstream Christianity among young Americans as well as a rise in occultism.

- Despite the rise in practicing witches, the U.S. is still dominated by Christianity, which composes 70 percent of the country's religious population, the Pew Research Center noted earlier this year.

- A little more than 22 percent of Americans list themselves as "unaffiliated" with any religion.

- The Pew Research Center, which has long pointed out the ongoing decline in U.S. Protestant and Catholic membership, released a June survey which found adults under 40 are far less likely to say religion is "very important" in their lives.

- "The rejection of Christianity has left a void that people, as inherently spiritual beings, will seek to fill", author Julie Roys said in comments emailed to The Christian Post last month. "Plus, Wicca has effectively repackaged witchcraft for millennial consumption," Roys continued. "No longer is witchcraft and paganism satanic and demonic, it's a 'pre-Christian tradition' that promotes 'free thought' and 'understanding of earth and nature."

Why are people turning to witchcraft and other occult practices? I believe that there are multiple reasons, all of which are dangerous for the people that are practicing witchcraft as well as for the intended targeted victims of their practices:

- People are unhappy and or frustrated with the adversity in their lives and they desire a quick fix to their problems. The adversity might even be caused by the same evil forces they choose to conjure through witchcraft and other occult practices.

- People may be simply naïve, intrigued, and tempted by bestselling books, popular films, and television series that glamorize witchcraft and portray it as safe and powerful.

- Naïve people may be pressured by friends to participate in witchcraft coven activities or occult practices for entertainment purposes.

- People may also be unaware of the dangers that result from practicing witchcraft, Satanism, and occult practices.

- The last reason is that many evil human beings exist, and they are fully committed to performing evil, sometimes in exchange for money, sometimes for entertainment, but always without conscience.

Satanists, sorcerers, and witches that practice witchcraft for the purpose of harming other human beings as well as people that pay them to do harmful witchcraft need to be held accountable to laws that prohibit these activities. There is a need to modernize and standardize our legal statutes to enable this at a state level and at a national level. There is also a need to train law enforcement and intelligence agencies regarding this criminality. Deliberate efforts to reduce and eradicate black magic in 2020 and beyond must obviously be executed in a professional, scientific, and methodical manner. Modern law enforcement and court proceedings must not resemble previous witch hunts, where the prosecution of witchcraft was primarily a ruse and a tool for persecution of political enemies, petty rivalries, and to oppress outspoken people. During these previous persecutions, thousands of innocent human beings were killed around the world.

The danger to the practitioners of witchcraft is that they are communicating with and conjuring spiritual beings in order to carry out their wishes, even if the naïve ones do not realize this, and the spiritual beings will demand something in return, such as submission to them and possession. One exorcist recounted a story about a woman who had escaped from a witches coven, and during an exorcism, the demon laughed about the misconception that witches have, which is the belief that they have any control with their spells over what demons do.

One of the things that I find interesting is how well people can successfully conceal their practicing of witchcraft and Satanism, even from friends and their community. They will go to great lengths to avoid suspicion, including regular attendance at a church or other house of worship, and socializing with people that do not practice witchcraft and Satanism.

I know a woman who has suffered from chronic pain for many years, and despite seeking treatment from specialist physicians several times, has not yet been able to find an effective medical remedy to her pain. This was the incentive for her to turn to witchcraft for a cure. On some occasions, she will appear normal and pleasant. On other occasions, when I happened to see her and asked her how she was feeling, she would say miserable and her facial expression and movements supported that assessment. However, when I would see her at a social event, she acted as if she had no pain at all and moved extremely gracefully. A few years ago, God told me that she practices witchcraft and her use has been expanded beyond pain relief. An interesting phenomenon appears to be a spell that I infer she casts in order to attract the attention of men to her. Even though her normal daily appearance is typical for a woman of her age, during evening social events, her appearance comes across as stunning. I do not mean stunning from the standpoint of a fancy hairdo, makeup, and designer clothing, I mean supernaturally stunning. I have seen the effects of this on other men, including married men, over several years, where they were uncontrollably drawn to her. I also had a rare personal experience regarding this early one afternoon, when I unexpectedly saw her while I was doing an errand. When I first noticed her, I felt my senses perk up and adrenaline go up as well, since she had a sparkle about her. However, a few seconds later, when I took another look in her direction, I noticed that the air around her seemed to have ripples in the same way that you might see air ripples in the distance above a road surface during a very hot day. This was not a hot day. Basically, what I saw was refraction of a kind that I had never seen. After noticing the aberration in the air surrounding her, I took a closer look at her and she appeared the way she normally does, and I also did not experience any physical reaction. Basically, in this case, the witchcraft causes an illusion and a somatic reaction, both of which are deceptions.

I'm certain that there are several people claiming expertise in the occult and demonology who may take exception with the above characterizations of witchcraft, claiming there are very different types of witchcraft, which can produce beneficial results and not just evil results. They may also claim that there are different types of spiritual entities and that some of these spiritual entities can be helpful to humans, even though they are separate from God's good angels. I do not believe that this is true. The important point that I would like to make is that everyone should refrain from witchcraft and occult practices. If you believe that you are a target of spiritual attack, you should contact your clergy of preference to discuss an optimal approach to remediation.

To reiterate, Satan and his demons do not want people to know that they are real, since that revelation would allow people to better protect themselves. The evil people that worship Satan and demons also do not want you to know about them, since exposure would make them ineffective and reveal their evil deeds. Furthermore, evil people that worship Satan typically conduct what is called a black mass, which is meant to be the opposite of a Catholic mass. They blaspheme God, desecrate the sacred host, and sacrifice both human and animal lives. Numerous times, I have been at a Catholic mass and heard the priest tell the congregation that the sacred host is not to be removed from the church. Evil people steal the sacred host for these black masses. I have seen video testimonies of former Satanists that escaped and told harrowing stories of years of abuse that they experienced and the routine murders that they witnessed during rituals. I believe that many of the missing persons cases, especially those of children, and many cases of human trafficking are due to these evil covens of Satanists.

In the Preface to the New Edition of his book, *Hostage to the Devil: The Possession and Exorcism of Five Contemporary Americans* (Martin, 1992), Father Malachi Martin mentioned several key points regarding the state of society and the activity of Satanists. He also mentioned this same information during television interviews and during radio broadcasts. I have summarized several of his major points:

- There are many Satanic covens in the United States.

- Typical membership includes people of all vocations, including physicians, attorneys, clergy, etc. Many of these same people also attend traditional houses of worship, such as churches, in order to help conceal their true allegiance.

- Black masses are held regularly in every major metropolitan area.

- There are Satanic covens with specializations, based upon sexual preferences, such as pedophilia.

- Large amounts of anecdotal evidence indicate that human sacrifice is an important part of Satanic ritualism, and members of a coven are sworn to secrecy. Violation of this secrecy is punishable by ritual death by knife stab wounds inflicted for each year of age.

- Coven concealment of murders and ritual sacrifices is made possible through portable incinerators and crematoria.

- Many babies are intentionally conceived and born for the purpose of becoming victims. No birth records nor baptismal records are kept in order to maintain secrecy.

- Cases of demonic possession have been on the rise.

- The increasing incidence of demonic possession of young children is especially disturbing.

- Cultural desolation brought on by lack of religious devotion, lack of critical religious education covering doctrines and dangers, a prevalent self-interest and materialistic mentality, lack of life mentoring, lack of prohibitions by parents and other influential people against immoral and unhealthy behaviors, disintegration of the family and the resulting trauma and aimlessness that results, and the lack of training and belief by clergy in Satan and the Forces of Evil, provides a fertile environment for Satanism to grow and the incidence of demonic possessions to increase.

- Law enforcement officers have seen a significant increase in ritual crimes committed, including murder, as evidenced by broken crucifixes, Satanic graffiti, pentagrams, and other symbols and artifacts. However, the availability of expert assistance for law enforcement has decreased.

Father Martin's comments are shocking and disturbing, especially for anyone not knowledgeable about this subject matter. In August of 2020, one exorcist shared with me that he had four cases of sexually abused former Satanists that escaped from their Satanic covens. They validated several of these points, including human sacrifice and cremation.

Based upon the increasing incidence of occultism and requests for exorcisms in Italy and elsewhere, Saint John Paul II, as Pope, in 2004, had the Congregation for the Doctrine of the Faith send a letter to the bishop of each Catholic Diocese around the world, starting with America, requesting the appointment by each bishop of an exorcist. The director of the film *The Exorcist* in 1973, and the film *The Devil & Father Amorth* in 2017, William Friedkin, stated that in 2014 the Vatican officially recognized 250 exorcists in the International Association of Exorcists. In 2015, the Catholic Register reported that the "once dying trade" now has over 100 North American exorcists. In THE TABLET article mentioned earlier, it stated that in February of 2018, the International Association of Exorcists had 400 members, including 240 exorcists in Italy. While this is progress, there continues to be a shortage of clergy trained in spiritual deliverance.

To conclude this chapter on a positive note, I will refer to Father Jose Antonio Fortea, whom in his book entitled, *Interview With An Exorcist* (Fortea, 2006), mentions the following: "For a Christian, fear of the devil is completely unjustified, for faith in God casts out all fear." He also mentions uplifting experiences of Saint Thérèse of Lisieux and Saint Teresa of Avila.

In her autobiography, *The Story of a Soul* (Thérèse of Lisieux, 1912), Saint Thérèse of Lisieux mentions a childhood dream:

"I remember a dream I had at that age which impressed itself very deeply on my memory. I thought I was walking alone in the garden when, suddenly, I saw near the arbor two hideous little devils dancing with surprising agility on a barrel of lime, in spite of the heavy irons attached to their feet. At first they cast fiery glances at me; then, as though suddenly terrified, I saw them, in the twinkling of an eye, throw themselves down to the bottom of the barrel, from which they came out somehow, only to run and hide themselves in the laundry which opened into the garden. Finding them such cowards, I wanted to know what they were going to do, and, overcoming my fears, I went to the window. The wretched little creatures were there, running about on the tables, not knowing how to hide themselves from my gaze. From time to time they came nearer, peering through the windows with an uneasy air, then, seeing that I was still there, they began to run about again looking quite desperate. Of course this dream was nothing extraordinary; yet I think Our Lord made use of it to show me that a soul in the state of grace has nothing to fear from the devil, who is a coward, and will even fly from the gaze of a little child."

Saint Teresa of Avila actually saw demons in her convent, and yet overcame her fear. She described this in her autobiography, *The Autobiography of St. Teresa of Avila* (Teresa of Avila ,1565):

"It seemed to me that with the cross I could easily defeat them altogether. So I cried out, come on all of you; I am the servant of the Lord. I should like to see what you can do against me.

And certainly they seemed to be afraid of me for I was left in peace: I feared them so little, that the terrors which until now oppressed me, quitted me altogether; and though I saw them occasionally, I shall speak of this by and by, I was never again afraid of them; on the contrary, they seemed to be afraid of me."

CHAPTER 10: HOW TO PROTECT YOURSELF AND OTHERS AGAINST EVIL

It should be reassuring that there are specific things that anyone can do as well as specific things to avoid doing to protect themself against demons. The things to do include:

- Be the best that you can be every day, being considerate and respectful of others, and being helpful when needed.

- Joyfully fulfill your responsibilities, whether family-related, job-related, or personal commitment-related.

- Pursue a healthy faith life, setting aside time for daily prayer, participating in your religious faith of preference, and obtaining spiritual guidance and clergy blessings as needed.

- Give thanks to our God of all creation daily, and request help whenever you need it. God listens to our prayers. God does not always respond to our prayers as quickly as we would like, and God does not answer some prayers for our own good. I will not deny that there is some mystery in our lifetime regarding aspects of faith, but as we develop a closer relationship with God, our enlightenment and understanding increases. God often has a vision for our life that is much bigger and better than what we envision for ourselves.

These are helpful scriptures:

Besides this, you know what time it is, how it
is now the moment for you to wake from
sleep. For salvation is nearer to us now
than when we became believers; the night is
far gone, the day is near. Let us then lay aside the
works of darkness and put on the armor of light; let us live
honorably as in the day, not in reveling and drunkenness, not in
debauchery and licentiousness, not in quarreling and
jealousy. Instead, put on the Lord Jesus Christ, and make no
provision for the flesh, to gratify its desires.

Romans 13:11 – 13:14 (NRSV-CE)

Children obey your parents in the Lord, for this is
right. "Honor your father and mother"— this is
the first commandment with a promise: "so
that it may be well with you and you may live
long on the earth." And, fathers, do not
provoke your children to anger, but bring them
up in the discipline and instruction of the Lord.

Ephesians 6:1 – 6:4 (NRSV-CE)

Finally, be strong in the Lord and in the strength of his power. Put on the whole armor of God, so that you may be able to stand against the wiles of the devil. For our struggle is not against enemies of blood and flesh, but against the rulers, against the authorities, against the cosmic powers of this present darkness, against the spiritual Forces of Evil in the heavenly places. Therefore, take up the whole armor of God, so that you may be able to withstand that evil day, and having done everything, to stand firm. Stand therefore, and fasten the belt of truth around your waist, and put on the breastplate of righteousness. As shoes for your feet put on whatever will make you ready to proclaim the gospel of peace. With all of these, take the shield of faith, with which you will be able to quench all the flaming arrows of the evil one. Take the helmet of salvation, and the sword of the Spirit, which is the word of God.

Ephesians 6:10 – 6:17 (NRSV-CE)

There are also specific things not to do, because they can put you at risk of attracting demonic attention:

- Refrain from any occult practices, including the use of an Ouija board, tarot cards, scrying mirror, crystal ball, and conducting astral projection. In addition, depart as soon as possible from any location where you discover that occult practices are taking place.

- Stay away from books on witchcraft and refrain from attempting to perform witchcraft.

- Stay away from and do not join witch covens and Satanic covens.

- Do not participate in seances.

- Do not go ghost hunting, seek paranormal experiences nor attempt to obtain evidence of the paranormal by visiting structures or locations thought to be haunted.

- Do not seek out nor pay mediums, palm readers, and fortune tellers. Many of the so-called practitioners have no special capabilities, and are actually practicing fraud in pursuit of money. Much worse are the practitioners who derive their information and capabilities from demons, and they will not openly disclose this. There are legitimate mediums and people with unique spiritual sensitivities, but their number is a small percentage of the total population that claim these capabilities. In general, the concern about practitioners is not knowing how they have acquired these capabilities as well as not knowing who is communicating with them from a spiritual standpoint. Everyone should be careful not to willingly introduce demonic activity into their life.

As written in the Old Testament in **Deuteronomy 18:9 – 18:12 (NRSV-CE):**

When you come into the land that the Lord

your God is giving you, you must not learn

to imitate the abhorrent practices of those

nations. No one shall be found among you

who makes a son or daughter pass through

fire, or who practices divination, or is a

soothsayer, or an augur, or a sorcerer, or

one who casts spells, or who consults

ghosts or spirits, or who seeks oracles

from the dead. For whoever does these

things is abhorrent to the Lord; it is

because of such abhorrent practices that the

Lord your God is driving them out before you.

In addition, you should:

- Abstain from taking illegal substances.

- Avoid any substances that you may be in danger of abusing, such as alcohol.

- Do not socialize with people, including current friends, that promote illegal substance use and substance abuse, such as heavy alcohol consumption.

- Do not socialize with people that advocate and commit antisocial behavior.

- Do not socialize with people that advocate and commit criminal behavior.

- Do not socialize with people that promote and practice witchcraft or occult practices.

- Abstain from sinful behaviors.

- Avoid unhealthy behavioral addictions and if already addicted, seek professional help.

Demons attack people that they determine to be most vulnerable and they feed off negative human emotional energies associated with sins. If you carry around a lot of unforgiveness and resentments from having suffered traumatic events and or emotional wounds, seek help and rid yourself of these unhealthy emotions. If you have difficulty controlling your anger, seek professional treatment as well as training for managing stress. As written in the Old Testament:

Like a city breached, without walls,
is one who lacks self-control.

Proverbs 25:28 (NRSV-CE)

If lust, jealousy, pride (or vanity), gluttony, greed or sloth are causing you problems or unhappiness, seek professional help to overcome them.

If you suspect that you or someone you care about is under demonic attack, there are helpful things that you can do, including the saying of deliverance prayers. I have listed several in an appendix to this book and others can be found on the website www.bringhumanitytogether.com. Going to religious services and atoning for sins is also helpful. If these steps are not sufficient to alleviate the suffering, seek direct assistance from your preferred clergy. Most clergy can bless and say deliverance prayers for people that seek their help, especially on a scheduled basis.

CHAPTER 11: REDUCING THE INCIDENCE OF SUICIDE

Suicide has become a leading cause of death in the United States and around the globe. According to the Centers for Disease Control and Prevention (CDC) *WISQARS Leading Causes of Death Reports (2017)*:

- Suicide is the tenth leading cause of death in the United States, claiming the lives of over 47,000 people, with someone dying from suicide every 11 minutes.

- Suicide is the second leading cause of death among individuals between the ages of 10 and 34, and the fourth leading cause of death among individuals between the ages of 35 and 54.

- There were more than twice as many suicides (47,173) in the United States as there were homicides (19,510).

- Veteran suicides exceeded 6,000 each year from 2008 to 2017 and veteran suicide rates are 50% higher than the general population.

- There has been a 33% increase in suicide since 1999.

- The United States is at the highest suicide rate recorded in the U.S. since 1942.

- 10.6 million American adults seriously thought about suicide, 3.2 million made a plan, and 1.4 million attempted suicide.

According to the World Health Organization (2017), close to 800,000 people die globally due to suicide every year, which is one person dying every 40 seconds.

Whenever a demon causes a human being to commit suicide, it is considered a major victory by the Forces of Evil, and the demon is rewarded. A demon attacks a person's mind and will torment the person with repeated emphasis of negative thoughts about the person to pummel their self-esteem. Furthermore, the demon will attempt to convince the targeted human being of the lies that no one loves them, there is nobody available to help them, and that tomorrow will not be better than today. The demon can both inspire and leverage other people's negative behaviors toward the targeted human being. These negative behaviors can include rudeness, acts of cruelty, bullying, and negative social media posts. If the targeted human being does not have a strong emotional support system and feels isolated, the downward spiral will progress. Unless help is obtained to alleviate the situation, the oppression and obsession will continue and potentially result in suicide.

If you are considering suicide, even if sporadically, seek help from professionals immediately. In the United States, at the time of this book writing, the National Suicide Prevention Lifeline telephone number is 1 (800) 273 – 8255, and it is toll free and confidential. The

Spanish language Lifeline telephone number is 1(888) 628-9454. People who are deaf or hard of hearing can reach Lifeline via TTY by dialing 1(800) 799-4889 or use the Lifeline Live Chat service online.

If you know someone who speaks or posts online about suicide, acts profoundly alienated or severely depressed, encourage them to seek help and notify someone that can help.

Parents need to engage children more to understand how they spend their time (socially and online), how they feel, and to identify signs of trouble. Signs of trouble include social withdrawal, feeling alienated, and frequent anger or despair.

Anyone who is seriously contemplating suicide must obtain proper care from a psychiatrist or psychologist. After medical treatment has been effectively administered, which may entail medication in addition to psychotherapy, and after available social network support has been engaged, such as from helpful family and friends and even a physician-recommended support group, it can be beneficial to consider having the patient commit to pursuing a healthy spiritual life. God tells me that Satan and demons are the leading cause of all suicides. Therefore, if the patient is willing to make faith an important part of their lives, that presents an opportunity to seek spiritual deliverance from the patient's religious clergy of choice.

CHAPTER 12: REDUCING SUBSTANCE ABUSE AND BEHAVIORAL ADDICTIONS

Substance abuse ruins many lives and is the cause of many deaths each year. It is a major health problem that must be addressed:

- According to the Centers for Disease Control and Prevention website in March of 2020, every day, an average of 128 Americans died due to an opioid overdose (including heroin) in 2018.

- Per the Journal of the American Medical Association website on February 11, 2020, deaths from heroin overdoses increased from just under 2,100 deaths in 2002 to more than 15,000 deaths in 2018.

- The US News & World Report website, on January 8, 2020, described that between 1999 and 2017, alcohol-related deaths jumped from nearly 36,000 a year to almost 73,000.

- Per the National Institutes of Health website in 2020, a 2019 nicotine vaping study found 25% of 12th graders, 20% 10th graders, and 10% of 8th graders vaped daily.

The following data is from the Substance Abuse and Mental Health Services Administration (SAMHSA, 2018) publication, *Key substance use and mental health indicators in the United States: Results from the 2017 National Survey on Drug Use and Health* (HHS Publication No. SMA 18-5068, NSDUH Series H-53):

- Approximately 19.7 million people aged 12 or older had a substance use disorder (SUD) related to their use of alcohol or illicit drugs in the past year, including 14.5 million people who had an alcohol use disorder and 7.5 million people who had an illicit drug use disorder. The most common illicit drug use disorder was for marijuana (4.1 million people). An estimated 2.1 million people had an opioid use disorder, which includes 1.7 million people with a prescription pain reliever use disorder and 0.7 million people with a heroin use disorder.

- An estimated 11.4 million people misused opioids in the past year, including 11.1 million pain reliever misusers and 886,000 heroin users. Among people aged 12 or older who misused pain relievers in the past year, about 6 out of 10 people indicated that the main reason they misused pain relievers the last time they misused them was to relieve physical pain (62.6 percent), and about half (53.1 percent) obtained the last pain reliever they misused from a friend or relative.

- 140.6 million Americans aged 12 or older were current alcohol users, 66.6 million were binge drinkers in the past month, and 16.7 million were heavy drinkers in the past month. For men, binge alcohol use is defined in NSDUH as drinking five or more drinks on the same occasion on at least 1 day in the past 30 days. For women, binge drinking is defined as drinking four or more drinks on the same occasion on at least 1 day in the past 30 days. Heavy alcohol use is defined as binge drinking on 5 or more days in the past 30 days.

- About 7.4 million underage people aged 12 to 20 drank alcohol in the past month, which represents 1 in 5 individuals aged 12 to 20.

- 30.5 million people aged 12 or older used an illicit drug in the past 30 days (i.e., current use), which corresponds to about 1 in 9 Americans (11.2 percent). About 1 in 4 young adults aged 18 to 25 were current illicit drug users. Regardless of age, the estimates of current illicit drug use for 2017 were driven primarily by marijuana use and the misuse of prescription pain relievers. Among the 30.5 million people aged 12 or older who were current illicit drug users, 26.0 million were current marijuana users and 3.2 million were current misusers of prescription pain relievers. Smaller numbers of people were current users of cocaine, hallucinogens, methamphetamine, inhalants, or heroin or were current misusers of prescription tranquilizers, stimulants, or sedatives.

People with addictions typically require psychiatric care and sometimes medication.   A support group is often critical to successfully overcoming an addition. Just as critical is the emotional support system that a person has, whether it is comprised of family, relatives, or friends. Addictions are very difficult to resolve, because once a person is addicted, it becomes a lifelong struggle for many of them to avoid their substance of addiction.

Addiction is a human weakness that is used by the Forces of Evil to get an addicted person to commit sins and crimes as well as to cause further misery for themselves and others. Satan and demons do not sleep, so they can afflict people suffering from addictions with oppression (physical suffering) and obsession (mental suffering) twenty-four hours a day. People with addictions that do not realize that demons can put thoughts in their minds and can also affect their physical sensations, making normal physiological reactions worse, are at higher risk of continuing their substance abuse and or harmful behaviors, and will typically feel helpless to overcome their addiction.

In August of 2020, an exorcist mentioned to me that methamphetamine, cocaine, and marijuana are often deliberately cursed by the same drug cartels that provision them for the purpose of expediting and increasing the addiction of their customers.

Separate from substance abuse, but sometimes concurrent with it, are harmful behavioral addictions, which also ruin lives and cause suffering and death. These addictions may entail gambling, fighting, domestic violence, pornography, and other deleterious activities. Each of these behavioral addictions require psychiatric care to help the addicted person to obtain personal self-control. Medication and personal management skills training can be helpful. However, spiritual guidance and even spiritual deliverance can be helpful and might even be required after the patient is stabilized and considered to be safe. A person with a behavioral addiction may be demonically obsessed or possessed, in which case remediation requires an exorcist.

If you have an addiction problem, seek help from professionals. The Substance Abuse and Mental Health Services Administration (SAMHSA) National Helpline telephone number is 1-800-662-HELP (4357), also known as the Treatment Referral Routing Service or TTY 1-800-487-4889 is a confidential, free, 24-hour-a-day, 365-day-a-year, information service, in English and Spanish, for individuals and family members facing mental and/or substance use disorders. If you know someone that has an addiction problem, encourage them to seek professional help.

If psychological, medical, and support group interventions are not effective against the addiction, consider supplementing care with faith-based intervention and practices. In many cases, deliverance prayer, penance, and healthy spiritual practices will improve the situation.

CHAPTER 13: COUNTERING LONELINESS CAUSED BY DEMONIC ISOLATION

Loneliness has become a significant healthcare problem. Compelling research has shown that loneliness is detrimental to psychological and physiological health. Forbes.com, in an article entitled, "Millennials And The Loneliness Epidemic", on May 3, 2019, shared these findings:

- A 2018 survey from The Economist and the Kaiser Family Foundation (KFF) found that 22% of adults in the United States and 23% of adults in the United Kingdom say they always or often feel lonely, lack companionship, left out or isolated.

- A 2017 Cigna survey found that 46% of Americans always or sometimes feel lonely and 47% feel left out. 54% said they always or sometimes feel that no one knows them well.

- According to a nationwide survey released in October 2018 by the BBC, a third of Britons said that they often or very often feel lonely. Nearly half of Britons over age sixty-five consider the television or a pet to be their main source of company.

- In Japan, there are more than half a million people under the age of forty that have not left their home nor interacted with anyone for at least six months.

- Loneliness is emotionally painful and can lead to psychiatric disorders like depression, anxiety, schizophrenia, and even hallucinatory delirium. But only recently have they recognized how destructive it is to the body. In 2015, researchers at UCLA discovered that social isolation triggers cellular changes that result in chronic inflammation, predisposing the lonely to serious physical conditions like heart disease, stroke, metastatic cancer, and Alzheimer's disease. One 2015 analysis, which pooled data from seventy studies following 3.4 million people over seven years, found that lonely individuals had a 26% higher risk of dying. This figure rose to 32% if they lived alone.

Psychology Today, in an article entitled, "Loneliness: A New Epidemic in the United States", on February 12,2019, presented these findings:

- MDLinx, a news service for physicians, reports "The newest epidemic in America now affects up to 47% of adults — double the number affected a few decades ago."

- The findings relate to adverse health risks such as higher systolic blood pressure, body mass index, and high-density lipoprotein cholesterol levels. Depression and suicide are also cited.

- Vivek H. Murthy, past U.S. Surgeon General, in 2017, spoke of loneliness and emotional well-being as major public health concerns.

According to the Health Resources & Services Administration (HRSA.gov) in January of 2019, in an article entitled "The Loneliness Epidemic", two in five Americans report that they sometimes or always feel their social relationships are not meaningful, and one in five say they feel lonely or socially isolated. The lack of connection can have life threatening consequences, said Brigham Young University professor Julianne Holt-Lunstad, who testified before the U.S. Senate in April 2017.

Social media can perpetuate or exacerbate feelings of loneliness. The American Psychiatric Association, in their publication, "Americans are Concerned about Potential Negative Impacts of Social Media on Mental Health and Well-being", presented these findings on May 20, 2019: 38% of adults see social media usage as harmful to mental health; 45% see social media usage as having both positive and negative impact on mental health; and only 5% see it as having a positive impact.

In May 2019, the American Psychological Association mentioned the following in their publication, "The risks of social isolation":

- Loneliness can wreak havoc on an individual's physical, mental, and cognitive health (Philosophical Transactions of the Royal Society B, Vol. 370, No. 1669, 2015). Hawkley points to evidence linking perceived social isolation with adverse health consequences including depression, poor sleep quality, impaired executive function, accelerated cognitive decline, poor cardiovascular function, and impaired immunity at every stage of life.

- In 2018, researchers at the Florida State University College of Medicine found that loneliness is associated with a 40 percent increase in a person's risk of dementia (The Journals of Gerontology: Series B, online 2018).

- In addition, a 2019 study led by Kassandra Alcaraz, PhD, MPH, a public health researcher with the American Cancer Society, analyzed data from more than 580,000 adults and found that social isolation increases the risk of premature death from every cause (American Journal of Epidemiology, Vol. 188, No. 1, 2019). According to Alcaraz, among black participants, social isolation doubled the risk of early death, while it increased the risk among white participants by 60 to 84 percent.

While every human being deals with some level of loneliness at multiple times in their life, isolation loneliness is a persistent case of isolation that can either be caused by natural circumstances or by deliberate preternatural actions. Not solving the isolation loneliness problem can result in bad situations and catastrophic events, such as low self-esteem, deep depression, extreme alienation, physical health problems, neurosis, psychosis in extreme situations, suicide, hatred of humanity, and violence, including the possibility of a mass casualty event.

By planting doubts and negative thoughts into the minds of the targeted individual and important people in their life, a demon can impair communications, create conflicts, damage relationships, cause loss of employment and resulting financial hardship, and have a deleterious effect on both mental and physical health. Lack of a healthy faith life increases vulnerability and risk. Once a targeted human is isolated, the human is even more susceptible to demonic manipulation, oppression, obsession, and possession. If the targeted human being is overwhelmed with sadness, the demon may attempt to convince them to commit suicide. If the targeted human being has difficulty controlling anger, feels great resentment in terms of how they have been treated by other human beings, and is frustrated to the point where they do not foresee a positive future, the demon may attempt to weaponize the human being in order to commit a mass casualty event. Demons receive the highest level of positive recognition from mass casualty events. One of the more distressing aspects of this, is that Satan and demons continue to focus on young, unhappy people that feel alienated in order to create these mass casualty events at schools, houses of worship, and other "soft" targets where there often are not armed safety officers and civilian firearms are prohibited. It is not uncommon before a mass casualty event, that the assailants will post on social media and seek to have a higher number of casualties than previous tragic events. It is also not uncommon for assailants to be involved with occult practices and Satanic worship.

Recognize the signs of isolation loneliness. Pursue help for yourself if you are suffering. If you know someone that is suffering, communicate in a caring manner with them, and recommend helpful intervention. If warranted, notify an appropriate family member or friend regarding your concerns. If you are aware of anyone that is a threat for committing violence, notify the appropriate authorities.

Every case is different and there are different causes for isolation loneliness. As mentioned, sometimes isolation loneliness is a naturally occurring situation, such as when a person must relocate away from family and friends for employment or when an aging spouse dies. If this is the case, promote healthy social interactions and activities. If available, enlist family members and friends to alleviate the isolation loneliness for the person affected. Help the person who is lonely to build a support system with social interaction: e.g. have them join and attend a hobby or special interest group, professional association, book review club, sports league or fan club, bible study group, etc. If a personality or behavioral disorder appears to be the cause for the isolation loneliness, seek a psychiatric evaluation, treatment, and counseling. If normal medical and social approaches do not work, be open to faith-based assistance and deliverance. Encouraging the lonely person to attend religious services and practice their faith can be a source of healing and inner peace as well as new friendships in the community.

CHAPTER 14: ADDRESSING PROBLEMS OF COMMUNICATION AND HATRED

Like most people, I have noticed an increase in communication problems and human conflicts over the past several years. They are frequently visible on television and on the internet as well as audible on radio and podcasts. It can include politicians at all levels of our government and between politicians of different governments. Poor examples of communications include polarizing, hateful, bigoted, and xenophobic speech, and they can also be found on any given city street, in any corporate office building, and too many other places. Everyone who communicates in a derogatory and hateful manner is part of the problem. Everyone who cares only about their own opinions being heard and not interested in anyone else's feedback is part of the problem. Just like we see in many political debates, which are characterized by unprofessional behavior, so many people seem to not desire constructive discussions. On the contrary, people with different viewpoints seem more interested in talking at other people as opposed to trying to understand different viewpoints in order to come up with a mutually acceptable and possibly advantageous compromise. In the United States, we have seen this frequently in the federal government in recent years, when decisions have been blindly made along political party lines, and the debates are typically vitriolic.

At the time of this writing, the United States and the rest of the world are dealing with the COVID-19 global pandemic, and it is admirable how some members of different political parties and different governments have been working more collaboratively together to remedy the difficult situations and widespread suffering due to the virus.

Indications of the problems that we have in communication and hatred include the following, which are having a profound impact on societies around the world, causing needless suffering, and needless deaths:

- Increased frequency of disrespectful speech and advertising across television and radio has impacted society and increased the tendency of human interactions to include anxiety, anger, and conflict.

- Deliberate weaponization of social media through the posting of fake news has increased social rifts and has generated violent reactions, including riots, murder, and genocide.

- The default emotions for many people resulting from the above seems to be frustration and anger, and this mindset is an obstacle to successful interpersonal communications.

- Polarization of views and attitudes also poses an obstacle for listening to and understanding interpersonal communications.

- People that choose not to listen to another person that is attempting to speak to them prevent their own ability to learn as well as prevent a collaborative discussion that can potentially result in a positive outcome.

Without clear communications channels, collaboration and compromise is not possible. The aforementioned creates a vicious cycle of increased tensions and conflicts. The results of this include:

- Human beings experience increased tensions and unnecessary conflicts due to prevalent negativism and faulty communications.

- The verbal conflicts we see daily in politics, business, and social interactions.

- The intimidation we see during international military situations.

- The tragedies caused by terrorism.

As mentioned previously, demons thrive on the negative energies of human anger and conflict. They also are vigilant for potential prey. Once they have identified a human target, they will observe behaviors in order to understand the target's state of mind as well as the target's "hot buttons", so that they can push them at will in order to cause conflicts.

The increase in hateful speech, particularly from government officials, has emboldened hate groups to become more visible and to commit crimes in public places. In the Washington Post article, "Recounting a day of rage, hate, violence and death", by Joe Helm on

August 14, 2017, a tragic weekend in Charlottesville, Virginia is described:

It started with a torchlight parade on Friday night in this normally peaceful college town. "Chanting, "White lives matter!", "You will not replace us!", and "Jews will not replace us!", several hundred white nationalists and white supremacists marched Friday as part of a Unite the Right rally at the University of Virginia that resulted in violence and three deaths the next day."

"The chants echoed as the group marched past the iconic halls of the university founded by Thomas Jefferson, paraded down the middle of the hallowed Lawn, climbed to the rotunda and converged on a statue of Jefferson himself. There they met their enemy. A group of about 30 (University of Virginia) students— students of color and white students — had locked arms around the base of the statue to face down the hundreds of torchbearers. The marchers circled the statue. Some made monkey noises at the black counter protesters. Then they began chanting, "White lives matter!" Within moments, there was chaos. Shoves. Punches. Both groups sprayed chemical irritants.

Many marchers threw their torches toward the statue and the students. Other than one university police officer, there was no sign of law enforcement along the march, and it was several minutes before police intervened. Both sides suffered injuries. They relied mostly on their cohorts for treatment until emergency personnel arrived."

Skirmishes between (white nationalists and white supremacists) and peaceful protestors continued the next day. In the afternoon, "rallygoer James Alex Fields Jr. allegedly roared his Dodge Challenger at a crowd of pedestrians. Heather Heyer, 32, of Charlottesville was killed, and 19 others were injured. Witnesses, though, had no doubt. It was "absolutely intentional," Matthew Korbon said as he watched victims being loaded into ambulances. He had been standing on the sidewalk. Korbon said he saw the driver plow into one group and reverse into another."

This series of events received nationwide and global attention. It highlighted the clear and present danger posed by white nationalists and white supremacists as well as the need for more proactive and robust intervention by law enforcement personnel and the U.S. National Guard.

According to the Miami Herald article, "Hate groups 'surge' across the country since Charlottesville riot, report says", by Charles Duncan on February 21, 2019, referring to a report by the Southern Poverty Law Center (SPLC):

- "Forty people died at the hands of what the SPLC called "alt-right killers" in 2018. The racist 'alt-right 'is still killing people, and 2018 was the deadliest year yet. The number is up from 17 in 2017. "

- "The number of hate groups in the United States is "surging," with the number hitting a record 1,020 hate groups in the United States.

- "Hate groups have grown in many states. In North Carolina, the number went from 32 in 2017 to 40 last year, according to the SPLC's new interactive "hate map." In Florida, that number went from 66 to 75 last year, and Texas also went from 66 to 75 known groups."

Hate crimes against people of several religious affiliations have increased in the United States and around the globe, including attacks against Jews, Catholics, Protestants, and Muslims. On October 27, 2018, in my hometown neighborhood of Squirrel Hill in Pittsburgh, Pennsylvania, there was a hate-motivated mass shooting at the Tree of Life synagogue, where I have celebrated many occasions. To many in the community and around the world, the unprovoked attack on the Jewish house of worship was an enormous shock. This type of terrorism had not been experienced before in the neighborhood nor in the Pittsburgh metropolitan area. This was the largest murderous act of anti-Semitism ever perpetrated in the United States. Eleven people were killed, and six others were injured. People close to me are still mourning the death of dear friends in this tragedy. While there have been many tragedies due to mass shootings, I mention this example to emphasize that an approach to preventing future tragedies is very important to me and it should be to everyone.

According to the Anti-Defamation League (ADL), in 2019, ADL recorded 2,107 antisemitic incidents in the United States, the highest number since ADL established the Audit in 1979. The high number of incidents came as the Jewish community grappled with vicious and lethal antisemitic attacks against communities in Poway, Jersey City and Monsey, and a spree of violent assaults in Brooklyn. The 2019 ADL Audit of Antisemitic Incidents found that the total number of antisemitic incidents in 2019 increased 12 percent over the previous year, with a disturbing 56 percent increase in assaults. The audit found there were, on average, as many as six antisemitic incidents in the U.S. for each day in the calendar year."

ADL's website further highlights the following: "ADL's research shows that the recent increase in global anti-Semitism is due to the triple threat of extreme right nationalism, extreme left anti-Semitism, often in the guise of anti-Israel rhetoric, and violent Islamist radicalism.

The ADL Global 100: An Index of Anti-Semitism, ADL's groundbreaking 2014 poll, revealed that more than one billion people worldwide hold anti-Semitic views. The poll surveyed 53,100 adults in 102 countries and territories in an effort to establish, for the first time, a comprehensive data-based research survey of the level and intensity of anti-Jewish sentiment across the world. More than one-in-four adults, 26 percent of those surveyed, are deeply infected with anti-Semitic attitudes. Of these people who hold anti-Semitic views, 70 percent have never actually met a Jewish person. This data can be extrapolated to represent an estimated 1.09 billion people around the world. The findings include:

- Only 54 percent of those polled globally have ever heard of the Holocaust.

- Two out of three people surveyed have either never heard of the Holocaust or do not believe historical accounts to be accurate.

- 41 percent believe Jews are more loyal to Israel than their own country.

- 74 percent of people in the Middle East and North Africa hold anti-Semitic attitudes — the highest regional percentage in the world.

- Three out of 10 respondents, 30 percent, believe Jews make up between 1 to 10 percent of the world's population. Another 18 percent believe Jews make up more than 10 percent of the world's population. 16 percent responded less than 1 percent. The actual percentage of the world's population that is Jewish is 0.19 percent.

A December 2018 European Union survey found that 80 percent of European Jews feel that anti-Semitism in their country has increased over the past five years, and 40 percent live in daily fear of being physically attacked.

In fact, attacks on houses of worship across multiple religions have increased in number in the last few years. To provide a sense of how widespread the problem is, these are additional recent examples:

- 2019: According to AP News, "Houses of worship attacked with deadly frequency in 2019", by David Crary | Associated Press,

    o On Dec. 1, a band of assailants opened fire on worshippers at a small-town Protestant church in Burkina Faso, an impoverished West African country where the Christian minority is increasingly a target of attacks. The victims included the pastor and several teenage boys; regional authorities attributed the attack to "unidentified armed men" who, according to witnesses, got away on motorcycles.

    o A two-week span in January illustrated the scope of this somber phenomenon. In Thailand, a group of separatist insurgents attacked a Buddhist temple, killing the abbot and one of his fellow monks. In the Philippines, two suicide attackers detonated bombs during a Mass in a Roman Catholic cathedral on the largely Muslim island of

Jolo, killing 23 and wounding about 100. Three days later, an attacker hurled a grenade into a mosque in a nearby city, killing two Muslim religion teachers.

o On March 15, a gunman allegedly fueled by anti-Muslim hatred attacked two mosques in Christchurch, New Zealand, killing 51 people. The man arrested for the killings had earlier published a manifesto espousing a white supremacist philosophy and detailing his plans to attack the mosques.

o On Easter Sunday, April 21, bombs shattered the celebratory services at two Catholic churches and a Protestant church in Sri Lanka. Other targets, in coordinated suicide attacks by local militants, included three luxury hotels. But Christian worshippers at the three churches, including dozens of children, accounted for a large majority of the roughly 260 people killed. The victims at St. Anthony's Shrine in Colombo included 11-month-old Avon Gomez, his two older brothers, and his parents.

o The day's biggest death toll — more than 100 — was at St. Sebastian's, a Catholic church in the seaside town of Negombo. It's known as "Little Rome" due to its abundance of churches and its role as the hub of Sri Lanka's small Catholic community. The attacks surprised many in the predominantly Buddhist country, where the Christian community totals about 7% of the population and has long avoided involvement in bitter ethnic and religious divides.

- o Six days after Easter, more than 9,400 miles from Sri Lanka, a gunman opened fire inside a synagogue in Poway, California as worshippers celebrated the last day of Passover. A 60-year-old woman was killed; an 8-year-old girl and two men, including the Chabad of Poway's rabbi, were wounded.

- o In October, more than 60 people were killed in a bombing during Friday prayers at a mosque in the village of Jodari in eastern Afghanistan.

- Nov. 5, 2017: Dressed in black tactical-style gear and armed with an assault weapon, 26-year-old Devin Kelley opened fire at the First Baptist Church of Sutherland Springs, Texas, killing 26 people and wounding about 20 others.

- Sept 24, 2017: Emanuel Kidega Samson, 25, was charged with killing a woman and wounding six other people with gunshots at Burnette Chapel Church of Christ in Nashville, Tennessee.

- Aug. 13, 2016: Imam Maulana Alauddin Akonjee and his friend Thara Uddin were fatally shot as they left a New York

City mosque. Oscar Morel, 35, was charged with second-degree murder.

- Aug. 9, 2016: A shooting during a party at a Jersey City, New Jersey, church left 17-year-old Leander Williams dead and two teenage girls wounded. Daequan Jackson, 18, was charged with murder.

- June 17, 2015: Nine black worshippers including a pastor were killed by Dylann Roof, a 21-year-old white supremacist, after he prayed with them for nearly an hour. The shooting happened at historic Emanuel African Methodist Episcopal Church in downtown Charleston, South Carolina. Roof was convicted of federal hate-crime and obstruction-of-religion charges and sentenced to death.

It is not difficult to find topics of controversy that trigger passionate discourse and expressions of hate. The history of the United States is complex, and it took many years to outlaw slavery, more years to allow women to vote, more years to ensure that minorities and people of color are legally entitled to equal rights, and more years until legislation passed regarding equal pay for men and women. Today, because of social media trolls, most of which are paid by foreign governments or other malevolent groups attempting to create and inflame social rifts as well as to manipulate elections, misinformation is widespread. Social conflicts and violence have been incited. There are inaccurate characterizations of political agendas spawning paranoia regarding fabricated government intentions. This fake news is incendiary and there needs to be better governance from social media and other news sources. There also needs to be widespread education of the citizens of many nations to help them to understand this dangerous phenomenon of fake news, how to exercise effective discernment, and how to identify trustworthy and credible sources of factual news.

I propose that hatred between good souls is illogical, unhealthy, and counterproductive for the following reasons:

- Hatred and resentment are unhealthy emotions, which increase stress, anger, and sadness, resulting in physical, mental, and social problems.

- The Human Genome Project informed humanity that all of us have a common evolutionary heritage, and that we have more in common than differences. This scientific accomplishment should be reflected upon and help dispel all human racist ideologies. From a higher-level perspective, there are two races that everyone should be concerned about: the human race and the race that seeks to destroy the human race, specifically demons. All of humanity has common enemies in Satan and demons, which seek to destroy all of us, regardless of our demographics and opinions.

- Human beings can differ in nationality, ethnicity, skin color, culture, tradition, music, cooking, and the arts, and these can be celebrated. Our differences provide us with synergies, especially during collaboration, and should not be the basis for conflicts.

- The one thing that a human being should have control over is their own behavior. Therefore, choosing not to hate and not to express hatred can result in better outcomes.

Here is a call to action:

- De-escalation is critical in stressful conflict situations to facilitate communications and to reduce risks.

- Seek first to understand and then to be understood.

- Active listening is key to understanding, learning, agreement, and harmony.

- I once heard that the following quote came from Thomas Jefferson after the Louisiana Purchase, which many historians consider to be the crowning achievement of his presidency: "Diplomacy is the currency of nations." In other words, we can accomplish better outcomes through amicable diplomacy as well as collaborative and productive negotiations.

I also believe that it is beneficial to keep in mind this Old Testament proverb:

"Death and life are in the power of the tongue, and
those who love it will eat its fruits."

Proverbs 18:21

CHAPTER 15: REDUCING GUN VIOLENCE AND MASS SHOOTINGS

We need to come up with effective approaches to reduce the widespread murder of innocents that is occurring in the United States and around the world. Both the quantity and frequency of gun violence and mass shooting incidents are alarming.

In the USA Today article, "Record wave of deadly shootings hits US cities. More police aren't the answer, activists say", by Trevor Hughes on August 15, 2020, it is noted that "Nationally, at least 11,047 people have died in gun violence so far this year, excluding suicide, compared to 15,208 in all of 2019, according to the Gun Violence Archive. At that rate, it will easily be the deadliest year for gun-related homicides since at least 1999, according to Centers for Disease Control and Prevention data. Community activists say the underlying causes of street violence will continue to fester unless properly addressed, and not simply suppressed by an "occupying force of warrior-cops," says longtime police reform activist Nkechi Taifa. Like other activists, Taifa argues that violence-prevention strategies have never been properly funded or given a chance to take root. Although many cities have anti-violence programs, like New York's Save Our Streets or Chicago's Cure Violence, they can be short-lived, poorly funded efforts when compared to the amount of money spent on policing.

According to The Washington Post, in the article, "2020 is shattering gun violence records. We must act." by Devin Hughes on July 21, 2020: "By July 19, the United States had already suffered 305 such shootings in 2020, including 60 in May and 95 in June. Those numbers smash records set just last year, as I lay out in a recent report. Previously, the most mass shootings ever seen in one month was 51, set in June 2019. Only seven months into this year, the United States has already experienced more mass shootings in 2020 than in either 2013 or 2014. The recent dramatic spike in mass shootings is part of a longer trend. From 2013 to 2019, the frequency of mass shootings increased by 65 percent. During that period, the country suffered 2,341 mass shootings that killed 2,642 people and wounded 9,766 more."

A specific type of shooting is called an Active Shooter Incident. As mentioned in the FBI's report, *Active Shooter Incidents in the United States in 2019*, the Advanced Law Enforcement Rapid Response Training (ALERRT) Center at Texas State University and the Federal Bureau of Investigation, U.S. Department of Justice, Washington, D.C. 2020, "The FBI defines an active shooter as one or more individuals actively engaged in killing or attempting to kill people in a populated area. Implicit in this definition is the shooter's use of one or more firearms. The *active* aspect of the definition inherently implies that both law enforcement personnel and citizens have the potential to affect the outcome of the incident based upon their responses to the situation. The FBI has designated 28 shootings in 2019 as active shooter incidents. Twelve of the 28 incidents met the criteria cited in the federal definition of "mass killings," that is, "three or more killings in a single incident." The 28 incidents resulted in 247 casualties (97 people killed, and 150 people wounded, excluding the shooters). The highest number of casualties (23 killed and 22 wounded) occurred at the Cielo Vista Walmart Supercenter #2201 in El Paso, Texas. The second highest number of casualties (nine killed and 27 wounded) occurred at the Oregon Historic District in Dayton, Ohio. These incidents were a significant increase over 2018.

Mass killings often happen in public places, especially where there are more vulnerabilities associated with so-called "soft targets", including houses of worship, schools and universities, and other venues where there is a lack of armed security, and where civilians are not permitted to carry firearms for self-defense. Terrorists intentionally target these places. By terrorist, I am referring to any human being that commits or would commit this type of heinous crime, whether they are an individual attacker or part of an organized hate group.

High risks are posed by mentally deranged, demonically obsessed, or demonically possessed individuals who have access to weapons that they should not have access to. A major goal and focus of attention for demons is to kill as many human beings as possible without revealing themselves as the cause.

According to CNN Editorial Research on May 3, 2020, the following is a list of the deadliest mass shooting attacks in the United States in modern history. You will notice that the majority of these have occurred in recent years. "Because there is no universal definition of mass shootings or central database tracking them, this list is based primarily on media reports and may not be complete or representative of all mass shootings."

- **58 killed - October 1, 2017** - In Las Vegas, 64-year-old Stephen Paddock of Mesquite, Nevada, sprays gunfire on a crowd of 22,000 concertgoers from the 32nd floor of the Mandalay Bay Resort and Casino, killing 58 people and injuring almost 700. Witnesses say the gunshots last between 10 and 15 minutes. Officers breach Paddock's hotel room to find him dead. Authorities believe Paddock killed himself and that he acted alone.

- **49 killed - June 12, 2016** - Omar Saddiqui Mateen, 29, opens fire inside Pulse, a gay nightclub, in Orlando. At least 49 people are killed and more than 50 are injured. Police shoot and kill Mateen during an operation to free hostages (that) officials say he was holding at the club.

- **32 killed - April 16, 2007** - Virginia Tech in Blacksburg, Virginia. A gunman, 23-year-old student Seung-Hui Cho, goes on a shooting spree killing 32 people in two locations and wounding an undetermined number of others on campus. The shooter dies by suicide.

- **27 killed - December 14, 2012** - Sandy Hook Elementary School - Newtown, Connecticut. Adam Lanza, 20, guns down 20 children, ages six and seven, and six adults, school staff and faculty, before turning the gun on himself. Investigating police later find Nancy Lanza, Adam's mother, dead from a gunshot wound.

- **25 and an unborn child killed - November 5, 2017** - A gunman opens fire on a small church in Sutherland Springs, Texas, killing 25 people and an unborn child and wounding 20 others. The shooter, identified by two law enforcement sources as Devin Patrick Kelley, is found dead after a brief chase, but it's unclear if it was self-inflicted.

- **23 killed - October 16, 1991** - In Killeen, Texas, 35-year-old George Hennard crashes his pickup truck through the wall of a Luby's Cafeteria. After exiting the truck, Hennard shoots and kills 23 people. He dies by suicide.

- **23 killed - August 3, 2019** - In El Paso, Texas 23 people are killed after a mass shooting at a Walmart store in a case that's being treated as domestic terrorism. Police say they found an anti-immigrant document espousing white nationalist and racist views, which they believe was written by the suspect, 21-year-old Patrick Crusius. Crusius is indicted on 90 federal charges, including hate crimes.

- **21 killed - July 18, 1984** - In San Ysidro, California, 41-year-old James Huberty, fatally shoots 21 people at a McDonald's. A police sharpshooter kills Huberty.

- **18 killed - August 1, 1966** - In Austin, Texas, Charles Joseph Whitman, a former US Marine, kills 16 and wounds at least 30 while shooting from a tower at the University of Texas at Austin. Police officers Ramiro Martinez and Houston McCoy fatally shoot Whitman in the tower. Whitman also killed his mother and wife earlier in the day.

- **17 killed - February 14, 2018 -** A former student unleashes a hail of gunfire at Marjory Stoneman Douglas High School in Parkland, Florida, killing at least 17 adults and children. Nikolas Cruz, 19, has been charged with 17 counts of premeditated murder.

- **14 killed - December 2, 2015 -** Married couple Syed Rizwan Farook and Tashfeen Malik open fire on an employee gathering taking place at Inland Regional Center in San Bernardino, California, killing 14 people. They are later killed in a shootout with police.

- **14 killed - August 20, 1986 -** In Edmond, Oklahoma, Patrick Henry Sherrill, a part-time mail carrier armed with three handguns, kills 14 postal workers in 10 minutes and then takes his own life.

- **13 and an unborn child killed - November 5, 2009 -** Maj. Nidal Malik Hasan kills 13 people and one unborn child and injures 32 at Fort Hood, Texas, during a shooting rampage. He is convicted and sentenced to death.

- **13 killed - April 3, 2009 -** In Binghamton, New York, Jiverly Wong kills 13 people and injures four during a shooting at an immigrant community center. He then kills himself.

- **13 killed - April 20, 1999** - Columbine High School - Littleton, Colorado. Eighteen-year-old Eric Harris and 17-year-old Dylan Klebold kill 12 fellow students and one teacher before dying by suicide in the school library.

- **13 killed - February 18, 1983** - Three men enter the Wah Mee gambling and social club in Seattle, rob the 14 occupants and then shoot each in the head, killing 13. Two of the men, Kwan Fai Mak and Benjamin Ng, are convicted of murder in August 1983. Both are serving life in prison. The third, Wai-Chiu "Tony" Ng, after years on the run in Canada, is eventually convicted of first-degree robbery and second-degree assault. He is deported to Hong Kong in 2014.

- **13 killed - September 25, 1982** - In Wilkes-Barre, Pennsylvania, 40-year-old prison guard George Banks kills 13 people including five of his own children. In September 2011, the Pennsylvania Supreme Court overturns his death sentence, stating that Banks is mentally incompetent.

- **13 killed - September 5, 1949** - In Camden, New Jersey, 28-year-old Howard Unruh, a veteran of World War II, shoots and kills 13 people as he walks down Camden's 32nd Street using a German-crafted Luger pistol. He is found insane and is committed to a state mental institution. He dies at the age of 88.

- **12 killed - May 31, 2019** - A shooter opens fire indiscriminately on a Virginia Beach city building, killing 12 people and injuring at least four others. The shooter dies at the scene after a gunfight with police. The gunman, later identified as 40-year-old DeWayne Craddock, was a certified professional engineer in the city's public utilities department for 15 years and had e-mailed a resignation letter that morning, citing "personal reasons."

- **12 killed - November 7, 2018 -** Twelve people are killed in a shooting at the Borderline Bar & Grill in Thousand Oaks, California. Officials say the gunman, Ian David Long, shot an unarmed security guard outside the bar, then went in and continued shooting, injuring other security workers, employees, and patrons. Long dies by suicide.

- **12 killed - September 16, 2013 -** Shots are fired inside the Washington Navy Yard, killing 12. The shooter, identified as Aaron Alexis, 34, is also killed.

- **12 killed - July 20, 2012 -** Twelve people are killed, and 58 are wounded in a shooting at a screening of the new Batman film in Aurora, Colorado. James E. Holmes, 24, dressed head-to-toe in protective tactical gear, sets off two devices of some kind before spraying the theater with bullets from an AR-15 rifle, a 12-gauge shotgun and at least one of two .40-caliber handguns police recovered at the scene. On July 16, 2015, Holmes is found guilty on all 165 counts against him, 24 first-degree murder, 140 attempted murder and one count of possession or control of an explosive or incendiary device. He is sentenced to life in prison without parole.

- **12 killed - July 29, 1999** - In Atlanta, 44-year-old Mark Barton kills his wife and two children at his home. He then opens fire in two different brokerage houses, killing nine people and wounding 12. He later kills himself.

- **11 killed - October 27, 2018** - Eleven people are killed in a shooting at the Tree of Life synagogue in the Squirrel Hill neighborhood of Pittsburgh. 46-year-old Robert Bowers surrenders to authorities on the third floor of the building and is now facing federal charges, including hate crimes. Bowers told a SWAT officer while receiving medical care that he wanted all Jews to die and that Jews "were committing genocide to his people," a criminal complaint filed in Allegheny County says.

- **10 Killed - May 18, 2018** - Dimitrios Pagourtzis, 17, allegedly walks into an art class and begins firing, killing eight students and two teachers at Santa Fe High School in Santa Fe, Texas. Pagourtzis is arrested and charged with capital murder and aggravated assault of a public servant.

- **10 killed - March 10, 2009** - In Alabama, Michael McLendon of Kinston, kills 10 and himself. The dead include his mother, grandparents, aunt, and uncle.

Sources: CNN, The Washington Post, The New York Times, Hartford Courant (Connecticut), Patriot News (Pennsylvania), Long Beach Press—Telegram (California), Richmond Times— Dispatch (Virginia), Fayetteville Observer (North Carolina),

Omaha World-Herald (Nebraska), Los Angeles Times, Chicago Tribune, Arizona Republic

According to FBI statistics, within the United States, police are typically onsite within four minutes. Four minutes is widely considered an expedient onsite response time for police as well as emergency medical services, which includes ambulance squad personnel and firefighters. Unfortunately, in most of the mass shooting cases to date, the killing is over within four minutes. Therefore, actions to protect innocents must start as soon as a threat is recognized. It is not hard to deduce that this is a problem that needs to be addressed more effectively than it has been to date. So, what can be done to reduce risk and reduce the casualties of these types of terrorist acts?

The following approaches may help:

- Sufficiently funded and promoted community violence-prevention programs. Too often, these programs are underfunded.

- Increased availability of psychological counseling and conflict resolution resources for communities at risk.

- Increased vigilance by the public with timely reporting to law enforcement regarding any individual of any age that speaks about or posts content on the internet regarding plans to do violence can prevent tragedy.

- Harden soft targets with trained security professionals. For locations without financial resources to hire trained security professionals, consider screened and trained teams of employees or screened and trained teams of volunteers for the hours per day when security is required. Adding physical security devices and surveillance equipment can also be beneficial.

- Active shooter readiness and first aid training should be conducted for all employers, employees, and regular attendees at all employer facilities, including schools. This training should cover not only tactics to protect people and minimize risk but should also include emergency care training for civilians. While there are multiple sources for first aid training, the American Red Cross Adult and Pediatric CPR/AED and First Aid course and First Aid for Severe Trauma (FAST) course are available. FAST was developed in collaboration with the National Center for Disaster Medicine and Public Health with grant support from the Department of Homeland Security Science and Technology Directorate. By the way, FAST will be offered to high school students at no charge, due to the grant. There is also professional training available from multiple sources for active shooter readiness. In addition, there is an acclaimed training video entitled "*Run. Hide. Fight.* ®, which is a registered trademark of the City of Houston. You can access this video and additional information at this website: http://houstontx.gov/oem/pages/preparedness/hazards/active-shooter.html

- Increased proactive monitoring by law enforcement and intelligence agencies of religious extremists, ultranationalists, and racist hate group members can identify those individuals that are most likely to commit heinous crimes.

- Increased implementation of video surveillance and professional security monitoring with software that detects known criminals, known hate group members, and weapons can provide an early warning system for law enforcement and potential targets. For example, if one or more individuals are approaching a school property and the software detects a known dangerous person, local law enforcement can be notified and the administration of the school can be notified so that a lockdown and other safety measures can be initiated. I recognize that there are widespread concerns about privacy and security when it comes to security cameras and government monitoring due to the fact that certain governments with poor human rights records use surveillance for population control, but we need to weigh the balance between safety and privacy, and have productive discussions and potentially even voting by the public. There are governments today with excellent human rights records, which have effectively deployed surveillance technology to protect their citizens. Funding and staffing are additional important items for discussion.

CHAPTER 16: A SOLUTION TO PREVENT NUCLEAR WAR

At the time of this writing, there is much division within the United States, particularly of a political nature, and there is also dangerous and unwise rhetoric directed at both our allies and potential adversaries. Since the Forces of Evil have a primary goal to maximize loss of human life, the most effective means to achieving this is by inciting a global war with nuclear weapons. The risks for war are numerous and high. The nations currently with conflicting goals and priorities are many, including the United States, Russia, China, North Korea, Iran, etc. The harsh rhetoric and lack of diplomacy between these nations increases the risks for conflict.

In order to alleviate the current conflicts and tensions, we need to create a consensus among nations based upon our unity against our common enemies, Satan and his demons, as well as a concerted focus on establishing our mutually beneficial and common goals. Historically, the fastest way to unite human beings is against a common enemy and around a common cause. With our new proof that God and Satan are real, we have an unprecedented opportunity to establish international collaboration for the benefit of humanity. In order to be successful, it will require leaders of all nations to practice the true art of diplomacy and jettison the saber-rattling rhetoric of recent years. We need to get away from competitive and imperialist mindsets, and realize that, especially due to existential threats, we either have the opportunity to collaborate successfully to create a safer and better world or most of us will perish in the foreseeable future. That is why I am here and writing this book. God desires a voice of reason to show mankind that there is a better way as well as a way out of our current predicament. God receives all of the glory for this, not me. No one will win if a global nuclear war breaks out. Therefore, we need to eliminate all risks of this happening.

As an international community, we must work together to solve major problems and improve the quality of life for all. Imagine the progress that can be made if nations did not need to worry about military attacks from other nations. If military forces can be focused on preventing terrorist attacks and proactively working on other risks to society, that will be extremely beneficial. Consider the benefits resulting from vast military resources and logistics being focused on humanitarian efforts and proactively ready to respond to the increasing number of natural disasters. Alleviating the current arms race will also free up at least hundreds of billions of dollars, which can be wisely invested to resolve existential problems and address other major problems as well. While there will always be a relatively small number of difficult personalities that are against peace and have their personal motivations for this, I am convinced that most human beings desire to live in peace and have their lives as well as the lives of those they care about to be joyful, filled with attractive opportunities, and hope for the future. Working together as an international community, we can make this a reality.

Therefore, we need this call to action:

- To all Leaders of Nations and Military Forces:

  - Implement diplomacy and de-escalation of tensions.

  - Outlaw and aggressively pursue all those that plan and conduct terrorism.

  - For those nations that have not already done so, cease all funding and support of terrorist organizations, including organizations that conduct cyberterrorism.

  - Outlaw and pursue organizations that disseminate fake news and other misinformation.

  - Establish proactive plans and readiness teams to help humanity (e.g. disaster response, special conservation projects, anti-terrorist operations, etc.).

- To civilians of all nations:

  - Promote peace through your words and actions.

Some of the benefits of our new international peace and collaboration will include:

1. Greatly reduced risk of war and terrorism.

2. Concerted efforts and synergies for the prioritization and remediation of existential threats and other global problems.

3. Improved relations and alleviation of international trade conflicts.

4. More financial investment options and more access to capital for investments.

5. Improved quality of life for many people suffering in the world.

CHAPTER 17: SOLVING THE WORLD'S PROBLEMS BY BRINGING HUMANITY TOGETHER

Many of the major problems faced by humanity require a global approach: e.g. climate change, plastics pollution, antibiotic resistant infections, unemployment and underemployment, proactive pandemic preparation, hunger and starvation, lack of population access to fresh water, terrorism, cyberterrorism, hate groups, etc. Entire books have been written and more can be written on each of these problems. We can make major progress on each of these with unprecedented international collaboration. I would like to briefly comment on the first four.

By establishing a commitment to international peace and collaboration, we will acquire enormous momentum to resolve our most pressing problems. Establishing expert teams within each nation as well as on an international basis along with empowered governance and accountability will be the first step toward tackling each of the global problems.

Climate change is a very real existential threat and has been globally recognized by the most accomplished scientists for many years. We need more nations to step up and do their share of improving the situation, especially those nations that continue to be major sources of greenhouse gases.

Plastics pollution is a more recently recognized existential threat. Giant collections of plastic garbage have been found throughout our oceans. The garbage is also found in many rivers near cities. The plastic garbage in our waterways kills many animals and so does the garbage that washes up on shore. Plastics disintegrate into very small pieces and are found in formerly pristine ocean areas. More foreboding is that many very small plastic pieces have been found on the deepest portions of the ocean floor, including the Mariana Trench. The ocean food chain ingests these plastic pieces, which include carcinogenic substances, and the concentration increases as we move up the food chain. By the time that humans consume the seafood, the concentration of pollutants is at its maximum. As time goes by, the situation gets worse. We need research to monitor the impact of plastics pollution on the food chain and on human beings. We also need to greatly expand upon the few successful projects to remove plastics pollution from our oceans and shorelines, although those efforts only skim the surface. The larger efforts to undertake include large scale education of citizens on the existential danger of plastics pollution, and more concentrated government and law enforcement focus in order to prevent further illegal dumping of plastic garbage into our waterways. We also need an intensely focused nationwide and international effort to come up with improved, practical, and affordable recycling of plastic garbage, since only a small percentage of recycling is taking place, and most plastic garbage on land is dumped into landfills, compounding a separate landfill problem. We need research to identify alternative packaging products that quickly and naturally decompose without negative environmental impact. There has been some successful research and development in this area, but it needs to be greatly expanded and implemented.

Another threat to humanity is the rise in antibiotic resistant infections, the misuse of antibiotics that exacerbates the situation, and the lack of research and development to create new effective antibiotics. A major reason for the lack of research and development is that pharmaceutical companies must invest a large amount of capital and resources to create a new drug, but new antibiotics are not a source of major profit. Therefore, we need governments to foster and support this critical new antibiotic development before catastrophe strikes. I envision an international partnership helping to expedite progress in this area. The recent international collaboration to come up with a COVID-19 vaccine has been encouraging to date, and an effective vaccine is expected years ahead of a typical development schedule. Significant government investment has already started. The pharmaceutical companies involved are willing to provide the vaccine at close to cost for the public benefit. It is truly admirable and shows humanity at our best!

Unemployment and underemployment are not only problems within nations, but international problems as well. Before the COVID-19 pandemic, unemployment in some countries was already high, especially for the age group segment under 30 years of age. Their talents are not bringing benefits to themselves nor others. In addition, these young people, if they do not have or do not perceive that they have access to sustainable employment, may become deliberate targets for recruiting by terrorist and other criminal organizations. We need to implement free (when possible) or affordable skills training resources on a nationwide and international basis that can provide hope for the unemployed and underemployed of our world. A lot can be accomplished by leveraging videoconferencing and video training over the internet. My career background has been in information technology and there are always labor skills shortages since technology is ever-changing. One benefit of application development, systems administration, technical support, and several other careers in information technology is that the work can be delivered virtually, that is, from a home office or wherever the employee is based and has internet access. There are many other skills outside of information technology that can be learned and delivered over an internet connection. I believe that a more concerted outreach to the unemployed segment of our population can open the door for improving lives by providing sustainable incomes, satisfying work, and alleviation of employer skills shortages on a nationwide and international basis.

Benefits of international collaboration include:

- More expedient progress addressing existential threats and other major problems.

- Inspired and accelerated innovation across technologies and processes.

- Improved preparedness for future crises.

As previously mentioned, Satan and his demons are very active enemies working against humanity and do not want us to solve these problems. Therefore, we should expect them to continue to attempt to prevent our progress with manipulations of key people in order to create political conflicts as well as to foster corruption. This should not be a source of long-term conflicts, since where evil abounds, God's Grace does much more abound. Working together in good will and being faithful will enable us to overcome this adversity.

CHAPTER 18: IMPLICATIONS FOR PHYSICAL HEALTHCARE

The main implication for physical healthcare is this: if evidence-based protocols are not effective in remediating an illness or condition, and there is no logical scientific explanation for the medical treatment failing, then it is best to supplement the medical care with spiritual intervention. This intervention should include prayers for healing by the patient, the patient's loved ones, clergy of the patient's choice, and professional healthcare workers that are caring for the patient. These healthcare providers can say their prayers in privacy or in the presence of the patient, depending upon their preference. This may be controversial for healthcare providers that refuse to publicly share expressions of their faith, because many are trained in school to maintain emotional distance from patients. They may also have healthcare management that looks down on religion or discourages this type of expression in front of a patient. Worse, as in any profession, there are a small number of practitioners with huge egos that behave as though they believe they are God.

I used to be skeptical about the claim that demons can cause physical ailments, which I read about in several books written by exorcists and heard about on numerous videos. However, having firsthand experience due to demonic physical attacks on me on at least four occasions, I can say with authority that they can cause great physical suffering, and I have no doubt that they can not only cause serious ailments, but also death. That being said, there are effective prayers that can be said and sacramentals that can be administered in order to counter the demonic attacks and alleviate the suffering.

Father Gabriele Amorth mentions examples in his book *An Exorcist Tells His Story*, (Amorth, 1999):

> "I have already mentioned that the two most commonly affected areas are the head and the stomach. Usually, the sickness is persistent. At times, though, it is transitory, lasting only the length of the exorcism. The latter include plague-like growths, stab wounds, and bruises. The *Ritual* suggests blessing the affected areas with the Sign of the Cross and sprinkling them with holy water.
>
> Many times, I have witnessed the efficacy of simply covering the area with the stole and pressing on it with one hand. Many times, women have come to me before undergoing surgery for ovarian cysts, which were diagnosed following a sonogram and the description of the pain. After the benediction, the pain stopped; a new sonogram showed the absence of any cyst, and surgery was canceled.
>
> Father Candido can document numerous cases of grave illnesses that disappeared simply with his "blessing", including medically verified brain tumors. I must caution that these incidents can happen only to people who are subject to

"negativities", and by this, I mean cases whose origin is of suspected evil origin."

There are many cases of miraculous healing chronicled over the years, that can reinforce our faith that God and the Forces of Good are actively engaged in helping humanity. In her book, *Medical Miracles: Doctors, Saints and Healing in the Modern World* (Duffin, 2008) physician and historian Dr. Jacalyn Duffin has examined Vatican sources on 1400 miracles from six continents and spanning four centuries. Overwhelmingly, the miracles cited in canonizations between 1588 and 1999 are healings, and the majority entail medical care and physician testimony. In an article reviewing this book, posted in the *Canadian Medical Association Journal (CMAJ)*, entitled "Making a case for medical miracles" (2010 Apr 6; 182(6): 595–596, Shelley McKellar, PhD, Associate Professor, notes this:

"Duffin says the Vatican placed increasing emphasis on medicine and physical healing in investigations of miracles. Over the years, it required greater medical testimony and detailed diagnoses. More doctors became involved in the investigations and more advanced technologies, from the stethoscope to imaging scans, contributed to the church's demands for greater proof of disease healing.

The types of diseases recorded also changed over time, reflecting shifts in disease prevalence in society and disease classification (nosology) in medical science. For example, the description of diseases such as tuberculosis, smallpox, malaria or simply fevers faded in the records as effective treatments emerged. Evidence of cancer or tumors remained constant, although its descriptor ranged from scirrhous, malignant ulcer or tumor to carcinoma and cancer.

One historical constant has been the key role played by doctors in the Vatican's investigation process. Physicians perform two important steps: They diagnose the condition as hopeless (a medical failure to cure) and they express surprise at the outcome (for which medicine could not take credit). When the Vatican is confident that doctors have exhausted the latest medical therapeutics and eliminated natural causes as an explanation, it can declare a healing miracle."

McKellar further states "So what prompted this self-professed atheist to become so interested in miraculous healing? Duffin unknowingly contributed to the successful canonization of Marie-Marguerite d'Youville, the first Canadian-born saint. Duffin confirmed severe acute leukemia — with a remission, a relapse, and another remission — in a living patient, who attributed her subsequent cure to the intercession of d'Youville. After that, Duffin says, she decided to learn more about miraculous healings, admitting that many of her medical colleagues were baffled by her research interest.

Duffin's study is good empirical history. She presents ample case narratives involving cancer, blindness, lung conditions, and other debilitating diseases. Based on her exhaustive research, Duffin challenges several historical assumptions, including that the Vatican was averse to the use of new medical therapeutics or technologies as standards of care. At a more mundane level, she explains the miracle record itself — what went into it, the role of doctors, the goal of Vatican leaders, and the lives of the people seeking help. Indeed, as Duffin suggests, these records are rich sources for religious, medical, and social historians alike. Regardless of whether you believe in medical miracles, Duffin's work should inspire further analysis in the convergence of medicine and religion."

There are several books that chronicle modern miraculous cures from the perspective of highly respected physicians. One book is *Miracles We Have Seen: America's Leading Physicians Share Stories They Can't Forget* by Dr. Harley Rotbart MD (Rotbart, 2016). The author's biography and book description on Amazon specifies:

"Harley Rotbart, MD, has been a nationally renowned pediatric specialist, parenting expert, speaker, and educator for over three decades. He is Professor and Vice Chair Emeritus of Pediatrics at the University of Colorado School of Medicine and Children's Hospital Colorado. He is the author of numerous medical and scientific publications, and books for lay audiences including *No Regrets Parenting* and *940 Saturdays*. Dr. Rotbart has been named to *Best Doctors in America* every year since 1996, as well as receiving numerous other national and local awards for research, teaching, and clinical work. He serves on the advisory boards of *Parents* magazine and *Parents.com*, and is a consultant to national and local media outlets. He is a regular contributor to *Parents* and the *New York Times.*"

"In this book, Dr. Rotbart has written a book of miracles— medical events witnessed by leading physicians for which there is no reasonable medical explanation, or if there is, the explanation itself is extraordinary. Among the extraordinary cases poignantly recounted by the physicians witnessing them:

- A priest visiting a hospitalized patient went into cardiac arrest on the elevator, which opened up on the cardiac floor, right at the foot of the cardiac specialist, at just the right moment.

- A tiny premature baby dying from irreversible lung disease despite the most intensive care who recovered almost immediately after being taken from his hospital bed and placed on his mother's chest.

- President John F. Kennedy's son Patrick, who died shortly after birth, and whose disease eventually led to research that saved generations of babies.

- A nine-year-old boy who was decapitated in a horrific car accident but survived without neurological damage.

- A woman who conceived and delivered a healthy baby—despite having had both of her fallopian tubes surgically removed.

- A young man whose only hope for survival was a heart transplant, but just at the moment he developed a potentially fatal complication making a transplant impossible, his own heart began healing itself.

- A teenage girl near death after contracting full-blown rabies who became the first patient ever to recover from that disease after an unexpected visit by Timothy Dolan, the man who would go on to become the Archbishop of New York.

- A Manhattan window-washer who fell 47 stories— and not only became the only person ever to survive a fall from that height but went on to make a full recovery."

The irony is that miracles are not rare, but they do not often appear in television news broadcasts, due to other news, especially bad news, taking up most of the broadcasts. In communities all across the United States, in emergency rooms, operating rooms, birth centers and delivery rooms, during ambulance crew and firefighter rescues, during police interventions and rescues, and many other situations, miracles do happen. Sometimes, God enlists people in the process of delivering the miracles and other times God works directly.

CHAPTER 19: IMPLICATIONS FOR MENTAL HEALTHCARE

Similar to the implications for physical healthcare, if proven psychotherapeutic approaches and pharmacological solutions do not alleviate the mental illness or condition, and there is no logical scientific explanation for why the medical treatment is failing, then it is best to supplement the medical care with spiritual intervention.

Mental disorders have different complexities than physical disorders. A mental disorder can also have a physiological basis. Examples of this include depression and schizophrenia. There can also be an emotional disorder basis, which can be caused by physical abuse or other traumatic experiences.

There are mental disorders that have symptoms similar to those that present with demonic possession. One example is the group of diseases known as schizophrenia, which can include symptoms of auditory and visual hallucinations. Additional examples include dissociative disorders. According to the *Diagnostic And Statistical Manual Of Mental Disorders, Fifth Edition* (American Psychiatric Association, 2013), "Dissociative disorders are characterized by a disruption of and/or discontinuity in the normal integration of consciousness, memory, identity, emotion, perception, body representation, motor control, and behavior. Dissociative symptoms can potentially disrupt every area of psychological functioning." Dissociative identity disorder, previously called multiple personality disorder, entails a condition that manifests multiple, distinct personalities. These different personalities typically differ in name, style of speech, different mannerisms, etc. Dissociative disorders typically develop as a reaction to long term physical and mental abuse as a coping mechanism.

A disturbing practice of Satanic covens is the abusive psychological programming of their members, recruits, and victims that are not sacrificed. This abuse is deliberately designed and executed in order to cause dissociative identity disorder. The goal is to cause the abused to compartmentalize and hide their abuse from the public and potential investigators, and to make it difficult for detailed recollections of abuse and to prevent credible courtroom testimony. The abuse is typically accompanied by threats of deadly retaliation against the abused and their families in the event that they report the abuse.

Patients with genuine schizophrenia and dissociative disorders can be treated with psychotherapy and medication. Generally, positive improvements can be seen. If the severity of the patient's condition is not too debilitating, they can lead productive lives. However, in cases where medical treatment does not bring improvement to a patient's condition, there may be additional causality at work. In this situation, supplementing medical treatment with prayers for the healing of the patient by the patient, if possible, by the patient's loved ones, by clergy of choice, and by professional healthcare workers that are caring for the patient may be helpful. If not, it may be helpful to consider additional spiritual intervention. If the patient speaks in a language that they were never trained in, exhibits strength well beyond what should be normal for their age and physical stature, demonstrates knowledge of things they could not possibly know, and exhibits intolerance for sacred items and places, then the patient probably needs the help of an exorcist. Obviously, if the patient's presence is accompanied by bizarre manifestations, such as major physical appearance changes and items seeming to be thrown around the room without anyone throwing them, there clearly is another presence in the room besides you and the patient.

Father Jose Antonio Fortea, in his book entitled, *Interview With An Exorcist* (Fortea, 2006), mentions that demons can continuously afflict human beings and cause a variety of mental illnesses, including obsessions, phobias, depression, etc.

Father Gabriele Amorth, who was the lead exorcist at the Vatican, told the story of a psychiatric nurse at a hospital in his famous book, *An Exorcist: More Stories*, published by Ignatius Press (Amorth, 1992). The nurse had been suffering emotional torments and nightmares for years. She also saw her coworkers suffering from mental illness and was afraid she would be next. Resentments and hatred dominated her thoughts and she was very concerned. In 1989, she met an exorcist by chance, described her suffering, and the exorcist recognized that she was under demonic attack, and was able to completely remedy her condition. She then introduced the exorcist to a patient that she thought suffered from demonic attack. The patient had been receiving treatment for fifteen years and some symptoms did not match the diagnosis. She accompanied the patient during visits to the exorcist and the patient's condition greatly improved to the point the original psychiatric diagnosis no longer applied. The nurse then told the exorcist about two violent inpatients that she thought may also be under demonic attack. Even though the exorcist never met with either of the two patients, he offered specific prayers for each of them. The result was that their violent behaviors vanished and the two patients were soon discharged from the hospital. The doctors were amazed by the rapid success of each intervention, but even the head of psychiatry did not feel comfortable attempting an explanation for any of these patients.

Obviously, professional discernment and a correct diagnosis is key to any successful treatment. Just because a person is hearing voices that other people do not hear or is seeing unusual things that other people cannot see, does not mean that the person is imagining the manifestations or has a psychiatric illness, because the manifestations may be indicative of demonic attack. Anyone experiencing these manifestations should seek immediate professional assistance from a psychiatrist for a medical evaluation and also should be open to the possibility that spiritual intervention may be a requirement to eliminate the manifestations.

Many people who have committed murders told prosecutors they repeatedly heard voices inside their heads telling them to commit the murders. Mass murderer, Ronald Joseph 'Butch' DeFeo Jr., who is associated with the Amityville Horror, was one who made such a claim. David Berkovitz of the Son of Sam murders also made such a claim. According to an article in Psychology Today, entitled

"Visionary Serial Killers Are Driven By Inner Demons", by criminology Professor Scott A. Bonn Ph.D. (1/26/2015),

"So-called *visionary killers* commit murder at the command of imagined internal or external voices which they experience and perceive to be real. Such individuals are often suffering from either psychoses or some other form of mental illness. Some visionary killers come to believe that they are someone else while others feel compelled to murder at the behest of entities such as the Devil or God. Both "God mandated" and "demon mandated" serial killers are fairly common and well documented."

He also wrote that "David Berkowitz told me that the FBI's version of their 1979 encounter is inaccurate. Berkowitz maintains that at the time of his murders he believed he was being ordered to kill by Satan."

CHAPTER 20: IMPROVING LAW ENFORCEMENT & COMMUNITY RELATIONS

Professional law enforcement is vital to ensuring order and safety in our society. Over the last few months, the United States news media has publicized a disturbing quantity of horrifying accounts of law enforcement personnel acting in a negligent, incompetent, and sometimes criminal manner. Several of these crimes, including three recently, were committed by white police officers on unarmed black people. Over the last several weeks, there have been disruptive and peaceful-turned-violent protests all across the United States and in cities around the world regarding the death of George Floyd in Minneapolis on May 25, 2020. Citizen-taken videos at the scene appear to show a deliberate murder by an officer that had the victim handcuffed and face down on the street as well as his full body weight on his back and neck. The officer's left knee was pressed down on George's neck for over eight minutes, which is almost three minutes beyond public perception of the victim becoming unconscious. During the police encounter, you can hear Floyd desperately vocalizing how he could not breathe. Another video shows that at one point, three officers were on top of Floyd's back while he was face down in the street, and a fourth officer stood by doing nothing to intervene. According to news stories, the police were called by a store owner because George handed him what appeared to be a counterfeit twenty-dollar bill. Floyd was unarmed. All four officers have since been arrested.

Back on February 23rd, Ahmaud Arbery, a 25-year-old unarmed black man was fatally shot while jogging not far from his home in a coastal South Georgia neighborhood. Arbery was intentionally followed by two armed white men in a truck and possibly by a third white male who took a video of the encounter. The white men claimed Arbery looked like a suspect in a string of local burglaries. No arrests were made immediately after the shooting, which resulted in protests. Only later were all three men arrested.

On March 13, 2020, just before 1 AM, three Louisville Metro Police Department officers executing a "no-knock search warrant" in a narcotics investigation, without uniforms nor body cameras, broke into the apartment of 26-year-old Breonna Taylor, an EMT, who had been asleep with her boyfriend. The boyfriend Kenneth Walker, was licensed to carry a firearm, and claimed that the officers did not identify themselves as law enforcement officers before breaking in. He thought the intruders were criminals executing a home invasion and fired shots in self-defense. The officers all fired back, and Taylor died after being shot eight times. Walker was also shot and was arrested. No narcotics were found. In April, Taylor's mother filed a lawsuit of wrongful death against the three officers, noting that a suspect (that) police were looking for had already been arrested by other officers executing a warrant at a separate location.

Investigations are proceeding in all three of these cases. The result of these tragedies, and several more in the recent past has been an increased degree of public concerns regarding the integrity, competence, and potential systemic racism of law enforcement personnel. There are specific communities that do not trust law enforcement and vice versa, which results in an increase in the risk that interactions can go wrong between the public and officers. There has also been an alarming increase over the years in the assaulting and ambushing of law enforcement personnel. In many areas, there is a need for increased trust, support, and collaboration between civilians and law enforcement personnel.

Satan's goals are to:

- Reduce public trust in law enforcement personnel.

- Incite civilian indignation and violence as well as encourage civilian lawlessness, looting, and overwhelm law enforcement personnel.

- Maximize destruction, death, and sinfulness.

These are important things for the public to consider:

- The overwhelming majority of law enforcement personnel care deeply about the civilians and the communities that they serve.

- Law enforcement personnel typically feel a calling to this profession and feel duty bound to protect and serve civilians.

In other words, they are not doing their jobs mainly because of the associated income.

- Law enforcement personnel routinely encounter dangers in their daily shifts and that impacts their perspective and behavior.

- For safe neighborhoods and communities, we need strong trust between civilians and law enforcement.

Below are several solutions to improving law enforcement and community relations:

- Federal and State governance mandating standardization of law enforcement training, processes, procedures, internal investigations, and reporting nationwide.

- More mandated and disciplined use of law enforcement cameras covering all public interactions.

- Prohibition of law enforcement excessive force with stringent oversight and rapid disciplinary action up to and including arrest of law enforcement personnel that violate prohibitions and the law.

- Enhanced firearms training and implementation of regulations that only permit law enforcement use of deadly force when they or other people are at imminent risk of death or serious injury from a suspect. Firearms training should include different skills and prioritization of those skills, such as first attempting to neutralize a threat via immobilization before an escalation of shooting to kill.

- 360-degree evaluations by management and peers to provide a balanced scorecard as well as to help identify personnel that have attitude, psychological issues, or behavioral issues that indicate that they should not be in their position.

- Community outreach by law enforcement agencies to nurture trust, build strong relationships, and ensure optimal communications with the communities they serve.

- Community representatives to work with local law enforcement and promote community trust and support of law enforcement personnel.

Here is a call to action for civilians:

- Show respect and consideration for law enforcement personnel.

- Promote friendly and helpful interactions.

- Be protective of your neighbors in addition to yourself and do not hesitate to contact law enforcement if you see suspicious people and or criminal behavior.

- If required, protect law enforcement personnel by calling for help or doing whatever you can do without endangering yourself.

The following is a call to action for law enforcement professionals:

- Treat every civilian with respect.

- Follow proven law enforcement best practices.

- De-escalate situations to reduce risks for all.

- Never stop training and enhancing your skills.

- Be the best you can be every shift.

- If you need psychiatric help, pursue it.

- If you need a change in position, pursue it.

- Management needs to remove personnel that demonstrate racist behaviors, have difficulty controlling anger, are the subject of numerous legitimate citizen complaints, and or use excessive force.

There are 17,985 U.S. police agencies, which include City Police Departments, County Sheriff's Offices, State Police/Highway Patrol and Federal Law Enforcement Agencies. According to the Department of Justice Bureau of Justice Statistics, in their April 2016 report, *National Sources of Law Enforcement Employment Data (NCJ 249681):*

> "Each agency has varying legal and geographic jurisdictions, ranging from single-officer police departments to those with more than 30,000 officers. The most common type of agency is the small-town police department that employs 10 or fewer officers. The decentralized, fragmented, and local nature of law enforcement in the United States makes it challenging to accurately count the number of agencies and officers."

This decentralized, fragmented, and local nature of law enforcement is conducive to lack of standardized procedures and processes, lack of higher-level oversight, risk of mismanagement and misconduct, and other potential risk factors. With improved governance, standardization, and a commitment to optimizing community relations, we will see significant improvements for both law enforcement personnel and the communities that they serve.

CHAPTER 21: AUTOBIOGRAPHY AND PERSPECTIVE ON FAITH

I believe the benefit of my providing autobiographical information will be to help you understand my background as a fairly normal if not typical human being as well as provide context for my evolution of faith prior to God commanding me to execute this rather extraordinary mission of bringing humanity together. There are, of course, many examples in the Old Testament and New Testament of God calling upon human beings to do extraordinary missions. Likewise, God is actively inspiring and working with many human beings today, most visibly in everyday heroes that protect and save lives around the world.

I was born in Pittsburgh, Pennsylvania, into a family with two twin sisters, almost fourteen years older than me, and one brother eight years older than me. My parents were both from Jewish families, although neither of my parents were rigid regarding religious practices while I was growing up. While all of my grandparents were raised in Orthodox Judaism in Europe and eventually practiced more of a Conservative Judaism in the United States, I would describe my father's form of religion to be Conservative Judaism and my mother's form to be Reform Judaism, sometimes called Liberal Judaism or Progressive Judaism. We lived in a comfortable duplex home, which was in the beautiful middle-class neighborhood of Squirrel Hill. It was close to a beautiful park, schools, and a vibrant shopping district. My family moved four years later into a larger home in the same neighborhood. It was a very safe neighborhood, and there was not much crime.

During World War Two, my father served in the Fourteenth Air Force (14 AF) under Major General Claire Lee Chennault, who had commanded the American Volunteer Group (AVG), better known as the "Flying Tigers". Several members of the Flying Tigers joined the 14 AF. When my father returned to the United States, he married my mother and worked alongside his father as a funeral director for a business owned by another family. My grandparents on my father's side lived above the Blank Brothers funeral home. My grandfather Jacob was born on a boat of immigrants coming to the United States from Lithuania. Jacob's mother and four brothers were from Vilnius, and his father died before the voyage. My grandmother, Ethel, was born into a family where she had twelve siblings. In the 1880s, her parents also arrived in the United States from Lithuania. Ethel was a homemaker and raised four children, two sons and two daughters. I remember Jacob and Ethel as very nice, but not very expressive in terms of affection.

My mother was an outstanding academic, having been one of the few women to attend Carnegie Tech, which is now called Carnegie Mellon University. A classmate of hers was John Nash, an American mathematician, Nobel Laureate in Economics, and Abel Prize winner. John was the inspiration for the movie, "A Beautiful Mind", a 2001 American biographical drama film directed by Ron Howard and starring Russell Crowe in the lead role. My mother became a schoolteacher for elementary school and Sunday religious school, and later became a substitute teacher for many years. She took time off from teaching to raise the children in our family. My mother's parents were both very warm and loving people. My Papa Morris was a kind and gentle man. He was a Polish immigrant who came to the United States and became a successful entrepreneur with my great Uncle Saul, who was the brother of my grandmother, Mama Dora. Dora and Saul were from the Jewish village of Plyskiv in the Ukraine area of Russia. They came to the United States before the Russian Revolution of 1917 after having survived several pogroms and murders by the anti-Semitic Russians in that area of Ukraine. I remember Dora tearfully recounting to me how on one day, the Russian soldiers rounded up all the young men they could find and shot them to death. Some of those men were only teenagers. Later, in 1941, during World War Two, the people of Plyskiv were annihilated by the Nazi's and a Ukrainian Police Force. I went to see a memorial for Plyskiv in Israel at Yad Vashem, The World Holocaust Remembrance Center. Unfortunately, my grandfather Morris's mother and sister stayed in Warsaw and even though he desperately tried to help them escape the Nazis, they were murdered at the Auschwitz concentration camp. My grandparents' experiences with antisemitism had a profound impact on me. Even though I was not religious as a child, I came to appreciate my Jewish heritage as special from the standpoint of the Old Testament, but I also had the understanding that many people around the world would gladly exterminate us.

We all need to keep in mind that there have been genocides up until recently, and autocratic governments are still unlawfully imprisoning and murdering citizens. The Nazi Holocaust was not that many years ago, from my perspective, and another holocaust could easily happen again if we do not take responsibility to ensure that it never happens again. The same hatreds that existed back then, exist today, both in the demons that promote hatred against Jews and peoples of all faiths, and the human beings that harbor these hatreds. As mentioned in a previous chapter, we have seen many recent attacks on houses of worship, targeting Christianity, Judaism, and Islam. We need to create a world that provides respect and protection for all good souls. The responsibility starts with each one of us, in our words, and in our actions.

Both of my parents were special people. My father was handsome, tough, a boxer while in the military, streetwise, and very charismatic. He felt very strongly that a man should have a strong work ethic, be self-reliant, and he was adamant that your word and the honor of your name are of paramount importance. He was not very expressive in terms of affection, while I knew him. My mother was more intellectual, had absorbed an incredible plethora of books of all kinds, was much more emotionally expressive, and more flamboyant. She was also very gifted in writing and language and she coached me and my siblings all the way through high school. Both of my parents were very articulate and socially popular.

My parents had marital problems before I was conceived and were separated at the time I was conceived. My father moved back in with my mother and our entire family lived together until my sisters left for college in 1966. My parents' relationship endured some rocky years, until my father moved out again in 1971, when I was ten years old. I remember the anxiety I felt when my father left, although he got a place nearby, and I would see him on most weekends.

As I look back on my younger life, I recognize that I had many spiritual experiences as a child, but I did not recognize them as such while experiencing them. I recall from the time I was seven until I was fifteen, I would occasionally have terrifying dreams with monsters. I recall sleeping over a friend's house when I was eleven years old and his sister awakened me early the next morning because I had been screaming. Having the benefits of studying child psychology as well as years of spiritual experience as an adult, I realize now that those terrifying dreams were not really dreams nor what are called night terrors; they were deliberate intimidations from demons. Another time, I happened to be riding my bike alone at the age of twelve, planning to drive one of my favorite trails in the woods of a nearby park. Many times, I had driven that same trail with friends. This time, I drove a little past the trail head and into the beginning of the woods, when I saw a very unusual sight: an elderly white-haired man in a fine suit and fedora, probably in his eighties but not looking the least bit frail, sitting alone in the middle of a bench beside the trail, and surrounded by countless bright white doves. There was a strange feeling in the environs that seemed to have a supernatural quality about it. I had never seen bright white doves in nature nor any doves in this park. Just then, I received an intuition that if I drove close to that man, I would never see home again. There was an overwhelming sense of danger, despite the scenery not indicating what most people would consider dangerous. In retrospect, I believe that there was some type of deliberate illusion concealing a physical danger.

I attended good schools all the way through high school. I was able to walk to school with the other kids. Back in the 1970s, at least in areas around Pittsburgh, especially Squirrel Hill, you did not need to worry about child predators and kidnappings; and you rarely heard about incidents involving them on the television news or in the newspapers. The world seems very different everywhere today, where adults need to be ever vigilant and children need to be continuously supervised and protected.

As a young child growing up, I was always fascinated by and passionate about science. I was a voracious reader, thanks to my mother taking me to Carnegie Library and the attached Carnegie Museum practically every week or two. I was very curious about nature, the world, how things worked, and I was not hesitant to question assertions. As a Jew, I was required to go to Hebrew school in advance of my thirteenth birthday in order to prepare to become a bar mitzvah. According to www.chabad.org, "Bar mitzvah is Hebrew for "son of commandment." When a Jewish boy turns 13, he has all the rights and obligations of a Jewish adult, including the commandments of the Torah." While I appreciated the importance of attending Hebrew School after my elementary school,

I was jealous of my friends who got to play ball on the playground while I was off to more school. Unfortunately, at my Hebrew school, The Hebrew Institute, which was a highly acclaimed school, my skeptical questioning was not always received well. I was the only child sent by my teachers to spend time in the principal's office, because I occasionally questioned their assertions of the literal interpretation of the Old Testament as historical fact.

Ironically, after having studied both the Old Testament and New Testament, the Dead Sea Scrolls, and archeology, I have learned that The Bible is repeatedly proven to be true as time goes on.

Even though I had a fun circle of friends when I was younger, I began to experience what I now recognize as demonic isolation. I had unusual difficulty creating new friendships as well as maintaining existing friendships as I got into high school. At the time, from my personal perspective, I did not seem to have any annoying habits nor was I antisocial in any way, but the success at relationship building that I saw that other kids enjoyed was something unavailable to me. I realize that high school years are tough for a lot of young people, but what I experienced was not only inexplicable to me, but it engendered huge feelings of frustration, sadness, loneliness, and at times, shame. By the time I was in my junior year, I was eager to move away from home and attend college.

Once I got to college, the situation changed completely, and I made many new friends upon arriving at the University of Michigan. After taking several classes, I realized that I had a passion for Psychology and for learning how to understand human behaviors. I studied Freudian Psychology, Analytical Psychology, Social Psychology, Neuropsychology, Child Psychology, Clinical Psychology, and Behavior Modification. I even got to practice therapeutic techniques that produced positive results for a long-term schizophrenic patient at Ypsilanti Regional Psychiatric Hospital to the great surprise of the staff. In fact, this long-term schizophrenic patient was able to move out of the hospital into an assisted living arrangement. Before I graduated, I spoke to the Dean of the Psychology Department about my interest in pursuing a career in Clinical Psychology. He immediately responded with a burdened countenance, informing me that I should not go into Clinical Psychology. "All of my friends are Clinical Psychologists and all of them are depressed. Instead, you should pursue the study of Organizational Psychology or go into the business world." I ended up taking his advice, leveraging the technical experience I learned doing programming and psychiatric research, and started my career with IBM in Kalamazoo, Michigan. IBM was the equivalent of graduate school for me, where I learned from thought leaders about best practices for major industries. I learned about process excellence and technology automation as well as the companies that implemented them. I went on to work in various roles in sales, consulting, and management for prominent large companies as well as smaller boutique organizations that specialized in consulting, technology implementation, and support.

Going back to the topic of religion, I did not become passionate about faith until my adult years. While I periodically attended synagogue with one or both parents when I was a child, I did not have a social circle nor anyone encouraging me to attend services through my teen years. After I started attending Catholic Church services at the request of friends during my college years, I derived a deep appreciation for prayer and giving thanks to God. I was inspired to pursue a deeper understanding of Christianity. Back then and to this day, I feel at home in every House of God.

After a downsizing at IBM in 1987, I moved to the Philadelphia area to be with my brother's family and close to my sister's family. A few months later, I met the woman who would eventually become my first wife. When I first saw her, I thought that she was a mirage, because she was so beautiful. She was Catholic and we attended church together. I had a few months of difficulty going forward with baptism, based upon my difficulty reconciling small portions of the New Testament that I perceived as antisemitic. However, God answered my concerns and explained the context for those depictions, and I was at peace about going forward. A few months prior to our wedding, even though I am proud of my Jewish heritage, I was inspired to become baptized and confirmed as a Catholic at the age of twenty-seven.

After marriage, my wife and I moved into a townhouse. Nine months later our first son was born. From the time we got married and for almost three and a half years, life seemed perfect. I do not remember a single argument nor unpleasant situation. These were halcyon years. My wife wanted to move into a larger home, and she found one she liked in Malvern. It was roomy with a large lawn, on a quiet street, and next to a cul-de-sac. It looked great. After moving in, my wife told me that the couple who had sold the property to us had marital problems, and also had behavioral difficulties with a disturbed and sometimes violent teenage son, who had "put his fist through a wall" in the house. Soon after our moving day, my wife started articulating various frustrations and tensions began to enter into our marriage. She thought that a carpet company did something against her wishes and she asked me to fix the problem. I was able to negotiate with the company management and they were so grateful with how friendly I was, they gave me free hats and tee shirts from their company. Over the next few years, while there were many wonderful memories with our son, our cocker spaniel, family, and friends, there seemed to be an increase in life pressures and marital tensions, which I was unable to explain. There were many occasions when our dog would growl and bark up at corners near the ceiling in the family room or simply stare intently at something that us humans could not see, which befuddled us time and time again. In retrospect, I wish I would have known back then about the concept of demonic infestation and the practice by priests of blessing a home. I have no doubt that would have helped the situation.

Within three of years of moving into the house at Malvern, I started attending Catholic Charismatic Prayer Group meetings. Charismatic means that there is a focus on thanksgiving and praise to God as well as a recognition of and celebration of God's spiritual gifts that he bestows upon chosen human beings. These charisms or spiritual gifts are mentioned in the New Testament by Paul:

Now there are varieties of gifts, but the
same Spirit; and there are varieties of
services, but the same Lord; and there
are varieties of activities, but it is the
same God who activates all of them
in everyone. To each is given the
manifestation of the Spirit for the
common good. To one is given
through the Spirit the utterance of
wisdom, and to another the utterance
of knowledge according to the same
Spirit, to another faith by the same Spirit,
to another gifts of healing by the one Spirit,
to another the working of miracles, to another
prophecy, to another the discernment of spirits,
to another various kinds of tongues, to
another the interpretation of tongues.
All these are activated by one and
the same Spirit, who allots to each one
individually just as the Spirit chooses.

1 Corinthians 12:4 – 12:11 (NRSV-CE)

The result of my participation included the experience of my being
"baptized in the Holy Spirit", which is a spiritual experience whereby
you establish a closer relationship with God. This experience led me
to be more faithful in prayer, attend more church services, and I began
to see success in more aspects of my life resulting from it. Ironically,

at the time, I was not familiar with details about spiritual warfare nor the activity of demons until many years later. The priests in the Charismatic movement that I met played down spiritual warfare saying that demons are no more than an occasional annoyance, and not to worry about it. In retrospect, this was unintentional misinformation. I was so focused on trying to be the best husband and father that I could be, as well as doing my best to develop and perform in my career, that I did not realize a slow and steady escalation of attacks on my marriage and the peace in my home. My first wife eventually told me, after the fact, that she resented my participation in the Charismatic Prayer Group as well as the deepening of my faith, because she had trouble with her faith due to a very difficult personal loss she had experienced prior to my meeting her. I felt helpless regarding how to help her strengthen her faith. We also started to see behavioral difficulties in our son, and my wife and I had different views regarding how to deal with it. There followed a routine of leading with my wife's preference of permissiveness and minimal discipline until things got out of hand, and then she would yell to me for help. We went through a rollercoaster of good experiences and arguments, the latter of which seemed unnecessary to me. The consistent feeling that I had was frustration not understanding why our relationship was deteriorating and heartbreak over the helplessness that I felt to improve the situation. Marital counseling did not help things, especially with a divorced marital counselor that my wife chose who had issues against men. I recall one discussion that we had before separating, where for the first time in a long time, we seemed to be on the same page in a very amicable exchange, and I brought up how the conflicts between us started with the move into the Malvern house with the presence perceived by our dog. There was about three seconds of us looking into each other's eyes and in total agreement. Just then, the dog started to bark, then the battery-powered fire alarm near us started to chirp, even though the battery was relatively new, and then the telephone rang, but no one was on the line.

I am not a "grass is always greener on the other side" kind of person. After I make a commitment, I live by that commitment. I prefer to make progress in life. In other words, when I take marital vows, I intend for the marriage to last forever. I felt completely helpless to save this one, because I did not understand what was trying to pull us apart nor how to fight it. We ended up separating in 1997 after five years in Malvern, finalizing a divorce two years later, and then getting an annulment from the Catholic Church.

My advice to any married couples that are having marital difficulties is this: remember what brought you together in the first place and how you felt back then. Realize how blessed you are to have each other. Love is about putting the other person first and not taking them for granted. Get objective professional help if you need it as opposed to giving up. Realize that marriage is sacred and because of that, there are evil forces that desire to pull your marriage apart. The motivation for these evil forces is not only to destroy the happiness of you and your spouse, but if you have children, the motivation is also to damage their faith in you, their faith in the importance and stability of marriage, and their faith in God. I have seen this too many times. For those married couples that I have known that chose to divorce, I have seen it negatively affect their children, regardless of age, even those children that are in their twenties and older.

I would like to share my perspective on faith, since I have found it to be a strong foundation for being successful against life's challenges as well as successful for combatting the Forces of Evil. I have written this book as a blessing to people of all faiths. Based upon my personal experiences; my Judeo-Christian background; my devotion to the doctrines, sacraments, and sacramentals of Catholic faith; my studies of the Holy Scriptures and demonology; and my real world battles against evil; I have complete certainty regarding the supremacy and unmatched power of God the Father, the authority and personal support of Jesus Christ, and the amazing capabilities of the Holy Spirit.

As it is written:

> Let the same mind be in you that was in
> Christ Jesus, who, though he was in
> the form of God, did not regard
> equality with God as something to
> be exploited, but emptied himself, taking
> the form of a slave, being born in human
> likeness. And being found in human form,
> he humbled himself and became obedient
> to the point of death — even death on a
> cross. Therefore, God also highly exalted
> him and gave him the name that is above
> every name, so that at the name of Jesus
> every knee should bend, in heaven and on
> earth and under the earth, and every tongue
> should confess that Jesus Christ is Lord,
> to the glory of God the Father.

Philippians 2: 5 – 2:11(NRSV-CE)

I have seen this in action, that when the name of Jesus is sincerely evoked with reverence and a request for help, evil backs down. From a scientific viewpoint, I am interested in all that we can learn about defeating the Forces of Evil. There are exorcists and demonologists in all major religions, and I believe that it will be beneficial for all of us to share what we have learned and what we have found to be effective. While I am curious about effective deliverance practices that recognize the God of all creation and do no harm to innocent people and animals, I prefer The Catholic Rite of Exorcism, based upon my faith, my familiarity with it, and the successful results. On a separate note, it is interesting to me that there continues to be debate within the Catholic Church regarding which version, "The Old Rite" (1614) or "The New Rite" (1998) is most effective. I find that exorcism practices vary by exorcist. Based upon a greater sharing of information and collaborative discussion, I believe valuable recommendations will be forthcoming.

Exorcism is a ritual of healing deliverance, whereby a demon or more likely, multiple demons are driven out of the body of a suffering human being. However, the demons are not destroyed nor are they made less harmful for the next human being that they attack. Not infrequently, the same demon can return to the same human being, and it may take months or years of exorcism before the person is fully liberated. It is also not uncommon for exorcists to encounter a demon of the same name in different people over time. In some cases, the personality of the demon seems to be identical to the same demon encountered previously, and that demon may even make comments about their previous encounter. Some exorcists theorize that many demons use the same name and consider their name to be more of group designation. By the way, the same demonic names are encountered all around the world. However, it is helpful to consider that when it comes to location and travel, demons are not limited by time and distance the way human beings are. There are many questions that need to be answered regarding demons. We simply need to share personal experiences and research findings in order to create a valuable knowledge base and data for analytics, so that we can come up with answers to our questions, optimal approaches to combatting specific demons, and potentially come up with innovative ideas for neutralizing the Forces of Evil.

I have heard certain Catholic exorcists speak with conviction that in many cases, for those people that are unwillingly possessed, that the result of the possession is that the person becomes committed to a diligent, healthy spiritual life that they would not otherwise pursue. They say that God allows the possession of the person in order to force the person to pursue a more spiritual and virtuous lifestyle.

One exorcist, Father Chad Ripperger, has spoken about many interesting topics on YouTube videos, and written several books. He interrogates demons at a point in the exorcism ritual when the demon is extremely vulnerable and suffering. One of Father Ripperger's assertions is that demons are on a very short leash, meaning that they can only do what God permits them to do. He references one demon that said that he entered and occupied the lower back on the right side of a person, because that was the only location that God permitted the demon to enter and occupy. Father Ripperger also states that another demon said that Hell was a place created by demons and not by God. The demon went on to say that Hell is a lonely and shameful place, where demons do not fellowship nor are supportive of each other, and it is a miserable place, which is the reason all demons fight so hard not to be exorcised from a human being.

The Catholic Rite of Exorcism follows a formal structure whereby questioning of the demons is targeted to specific information in order to understand how many demons are in the possessed person, how and when the demons got control as well as their entry point, what their names are, and what sign will be manifested when they leave the person. While all demons have an easy time telling lies, during The Rite, they are compelled to tell the truth, and they seem more credible when they express their suffering and are most vulnerable. A lot of what we know today about demons is derived from consistent information derived from multiple exorcism interrogations.

In terms of understanding my perspective on faith, I believe Father Gabriele Amorth described the "Centrality of Christ" best in his book *An Exorcist Tells His Story* (Amorth, 1999):

"The devil is one of God's creatures. We cannot talk about him and about exorcisms without first stating some basic facts about God's plan for creation. We will not say anything new, but we might present a new perspective.

All too often we have the wrong concept of creation, and we take for granted the following wrong sequence of events. We believe that one day God created the angels; that he put them to the test, although we are not sure which test; and that as a result we have the division among angels and demons. The angels were rewarded with heaven, and the demons were punished with hell. Then we believe that on another day God created the universe, the minerals, the plants, the animals, and, in the end, man. In the Garden of Eden, Adam and Eve obeyed Satan and disobeyed God; thus, they sinned. At this point, to save mankind, God decided to send his Son.

This is not what the Bible teaches us, and it is not the teaching of the Fathers. If this were so, the angels and creation would remain strangers to the mystery of Christ. If we read the prologue to the Gospel of John and the two Christological hymns that open the Letters to the Ephesians and the Colossians, we see that Christ is "the firstborn of all creatures" (Colossians 1:15). Everything was created for him and in the expectation of him. There is no theological discussion that makes any sense if it asks whether Christ would have been born without the sin of Adam. Christ is the center of creation; all creatures, both heavenly (the angels) and earthly (men) find in him their summation.

On the other hand, we can affirm that, given the sin of our forebears, Christ's coming assumed a particular role: he came as Savior. The core of his action is contained within the Paschal mystery: through the blood of his Cross, he reconciles all things in the heavens (angels) and on earth (men) to God. The role of every creature is dependent on this Christocentric understanding.

We cannot omit a reflection about the Virgin Mary. If the firstborn creature is the Word become flesh, she who would be the means of the Incarnation must also have been present in the divine thought before every other creature. From this stems Mary's unique relationship with the Holy Trinity.

We must also mention the influence that Christ has on angels and demons. Concerning angels, some theologians believe that the angels were admitted to the beatific vision of God only by virtue of the mystery of the Cross. Many Fathers also make interesting statements. For instance, Saint Athanasius writes that the angels owe their salvation to the blood of Christ. The Gospels give us many statements concerning demons, and they clearly state that Christ defeated the reign of Satan with his Cross and established the reign of God. The demons who possessed the Gerasene man exclaimed, "What is there between us, Son of God? Have you come to torment us before our time?" (Matthew 8:29). This is an obvious reference to the fact that the power of Satan is gradually broken by Christ. Satan's power, therefore, still exists and will continue to exist until our salvation will be completed, "because the accuser of our brethren will be cast out" (Revelation 12:10). Additional information on the role of Mary, enemy of Satan since the original announcement of salvation, can be found in the beautiful book by Father Candido Amantini, *Il mistero di Maria* (Naples: Dehoniane, 1971).

If we see everything in the light of the centrality of Christ, we can see God's plan, who created everything "for him and in expectation of him". And we can see the actions of Satan, the enemy, the tempter, the accuser. By means of his temptation, evil, pain, sin, and death entered the world. It is in this context that we are able to see the restoration of God's plan, which Christ accomplished at the cost of his blood.

In this context, we are made aware of the power of the devil. Jesus calls him "the prince of this world" (John 12:31, 14:30, 16:11). John affirms that "the whole world is in the power of the evil one" (1 John 5:19); by "the world" John means everything that is opposed to God. Satan was the brightest of the angels; he became the most evil of the devils and their chief. The demons remain bound to the same strict hierarchy that was given them when they were angels: principalities, thrones, dominions, and so on (Colossians 1:16). However, while the angels, whose chief is Michael, are bound by a hierarchy of love, the demons live under a rule of slavery.

We are also made aware of the action of Christ, who shattered the reign of Satan and established the kingdom of God. This is why the instances where Jesus freed those possessed by demons become particularly important. When Peter teaches Cornelius about Christ, he does not mention any miracle besides the fact that he cured "all those who had fallen under the power of the devil" (Acts 10:38). We understand, then, why the first authority that Jesus gave his apostles was the power to expel demons (Matthew 10:1). We can make the same statement for all believers: "These are the signs that will be associated with believers: in my name they will cast out devils" (Mark 16:17). Thus, Jesus heals and reestablishes the divine plan that had been ruined by the rebellion of some of the angels and by our forefathers.

We must make this abundantly clear: evil, suffering, death, and hell (that is, eternal damnation in everlasting torment) *are not acts of God.* I want to expand on this point. One day Father Candido was expelling a demon. Toward the end of the exorcism, he turned to the evil spirit and sarcastically told him, "Get out of here. The Lord has already prepared a nice, well-heated house for you!" At this, the demon answered, "You do not know anything! It wasn't he [God] who made hell. It was us. He had not even thought about it."

Similarly, on another occasion, while I was questioning a demon to know whether he had contributed to the creation of hell, I received this answer: "All of us cooperated." Christ's centrality in the plan of creation, and its restoration through redemption, is fundamental to understanding God's plan and the end of the world. Angels and men received an intelligent and free nature. When I am told (by those who confuse predestination with God's providence) that God already knows who will be saved and who will be damned, and therefore anything we do is useless, I usually answer with four truths that the Bible spells out for us: God wants that everyone be saved; no one is predestined to go to hell; Jesus died for everyone; and everyone is given sufficient graces for salvation.

Christ's centrality tells us that we can be saved only in his name. It is only in his name that we can win and free ourselves from the enemy of our salvation, Satan. At the end of the most difficult exorcisms, when I am confronted with total demonic possession, I pray the Christological hymn of the Letter of Paul to the Philippians (2:6-11). When I speak the words "so that all beings in the heavens, on earth, and in the underworld should bend the knee at the name of Jesus", I kneel, everyone present kneels, and always the one possessed by the demons is also compelled to kneel. It is a moving and powerful moment. I always feel that all the legions of the angels are surrounding us, kneeling at the name of Jesus."

Father Amorth's description is very helpful for anyone that has questions regarding Jesus, Christianity, and Catholicism. I find that for many people, especially for those who have turned away from religion, there is a surprising amount of confusion, misunderstandings, and even a lack of optimal foundation for their faith. There may also be a situation similar to that of several young people that I know, who studied and practiced their faith when they were very young but did not perceive associated benefits in their daily lives. Some of these young people may have been "going through the motions" to please their parents or other people and did not have an emotional investment. So many people are under the illusion that religion does not have a practical place in the modern world, that one's circumstances are not influenced by faith, but are simply based upon one's own actions and interactions with random events. I solemnly assure you that nothing can be further from the truth. I am hopeful that one of the results of the publishing of this book will be people rediscovering the importance of faith and that there will be a global revival. I also hope that the outcome of this will be unprecedented harmony and collaboration between people of all nations and religions.

CHAPTER 22: HISTORIC IMPORTANCE OF FAITH IN THE UNITED STATES

Since I am based in the United States of America, I thought it would be interesting to convey that religious faith has always been an important part of the history of this nation. I would like to share a few important items for consideration, since many people are unaware of the importance of religion to America.

The United States of America is a nation built by immigrants and their descendants, and new immigrants are arriving and enriching our nation on a continual basis. From the beginning, people traveled and often risked their lives to come to America to escape religious and political persecution. For these people, faith was a very important part of their lives. They needed faith to endure the long and treacherous journey across the ocean and across land. Most of these people had to start their new American life learning new farming techniques, new trade skills, and new survival skills. Life was hard for many of them. Unknown diseases were catastrophic. Nevertheless, they pressed on, building sustainable and prosperous communities over the years. Faith got them through difficult times.

As Charles J. Chaput, O.F.M. Cap., Archbishop of Philadelphia wrote in *A Heart on Fire* (Chaput, 2012), "…the American experience of personal freedom and civil peace is inconceivable without a religious grounding and a predominantly Christian inspiration. America was born, in James Madison's words, to be 'an asylum to the persecuted and oppressed of every nation and religion.'"

Fifty-three of the fifty-six signers of the Declaration of Independence were evangelical Christians. They risked their lives on a quest for and a proclamation of American independence. Patrick Henry, an American attorney, planter, and politician, famously proclaimed to the Second Virginia Convention, "Give me liberty or give me death." John Jay, one of the framers of the Constitution of the United States of America and the first Chief Justice of the United States Supreme Court, in a letter written to Representative John Murray on October 12, 1816, stated "Providence has given to our people the choice of their rulers, and it is the duty as well as the privilege and interest of our Christian nation to select and prefer Christians for their rulers."

Alexis de Tocqueville was a famous French aristocrat, diplomat, political scientist, and historian who wrote *De La Démocratie en Amérique,* which was translated as *Democracy in America*, published in two volumes in 1835 and 1840. When Tocqueville was touring America in preparation for these celebrated books, he was impressed by the hard-working and industrious work ethic of our people as well as their creativity. He was in awe of the beauty of our country and its vast natural resources. However, what impressed him the most, was when he walked into our houses of worship. He determined that "America is great, because America is good."

America has become the light of the world for human rights, liberty, lifestyle, and economic opportunity. It took a long time to get where we are now, and we still have a lot more work to do to improve in each of these areas. Recent widespread protests have shown that Americans are committed to getting rid of systemic racism and intolerance.

At the time, World War Two was the largest crisis faced by humanity. America and our Allies were at a critical point in what appeared to most people in the world to be a battle of good versus evil. Our enemies, known as the Axis, included Nazi Germany, Imperial Japan, and other collaborators, had committed atrocities at an unprecedented scale, and they were the embodiment of evil. It is noteworthy to mention that Adolf Hitler and many members of the Nazi leadership, including the military, were very active in and supportive of occult practices. Books have been written about this.

At 9:57 PM on D-Day, June 6, 1944, as mentioned on *The blog of the Franklin D. Roosevelt Presidential Library and Museum,*

> "Franklin Delano Roosevelt (FDR) sat in front of a microphone in the Diplomatic Reception Room at the White House waiting to begin a national radio address. FDR's address took the form of a prayer. He had composed it during the weekend before the invasion, with assistance from his daughter, Anna, and her husband, John Boettiger. The text was released in advance so Americans could recite it with him.

Roosevelt's "D-Day Prayer" struck a powerful chord with the nation. Printed copies were distributed and displayed widely throughout the remainder of the war."

The following is the text of FDR's prayer, which is as powerful today as it was back then:

"My fellow Americans: Last night, when I spoke with you about the fall of Rome, I knew at that moment that troops of the United States and our allies were crossing the Channel in another and greater operation. It has come to pass with success thus far. And so, in this poignant hour, I ask you to join with me in prayer:

Almighty God: Our sons, pride of our Nation, this day have set upon a mighty endeavor, a struggle to preserve our Republic, our religion, and our civilization, and to set free a suffering humanity. Lead them straight and true; give strength to their arms, stoutness to their hearts, steadfastness in their faith. They will need Thy blessings. Their road will be long and hard. For the enemy is strong. He may hurl back our forces. Success may not come with rushing speed, but we shall return again and again; and we know that by Thy grace, and by the righteousness of our cause, our sons will triumph.

They will be sore tried, by night and by day, without rest-until the victory is won. The darkness will be rent by noise and flame. Men's souls will be shaken with the violences of war.

For these men are lately drawn from the ways of peace. They fight not for the lust of conquest. They fight to end conquest. They fight to liberate. They fight to let justice arise, and tolerance and good will among all Thy people. They yearn but for the end of battle, for their return to the haven of home. Some will never return. Embrace these, Father, and receive them, Thy heroic servants, into Thy kingdom.

And for us at home — fathers, mothers, children, wives, sisters, and brothers of brave men overseas — whose thoughts and prayers are ever with them — help us, Almighty God, to rededicate ourselves in renewed faith in Thee in this hour of great sacrifice. Many people have urged that I call the Nation into a single day of special prayer. But because the road is long and the desire is great, I ask that our people devote themselves in a continuance of prayer. As we rise to each new day, and again when each day is spent, let words of prayer be on our lips, invoking Thy help to our efforts.

Give us strength, too — strength in our daily tasks, to redouble the contributions we make in the physical and the material support of our armed forces.

And let our hearts be stout, to wait out the long travail, to bear sorrows that may come, to impart our courage unto our sons wheresoever they may be.

And, O Lord, give us Faith. Give us Faith in Thee; Faith in our sons; Faith in each other; Faith in our united crusade. Let not the keenness of our spirit ever be dulled. Let not the impacts of temporary events, of temporal matters of but fleeting moment let not these deter us in our unconquerable purpose.

With Thy blessing, we shall prevail over the unholy forces of our enemy. Help us to conquer the apostles of greed and racial arrogancies. Lead us to the saving of our country, and with our sister Nations into a world unity that will spell a sure peace, a peace invulnerable to the schemings of unworthy men. And a peace that will let all of men live in freedom, reaping the just rewards of their honest toil.

Thy will be done, Almighty God. Amen."

According to Wikipedia
(https://en.wikipedia.org/wiki/World_War_II_casualties):

- "World War II was the deadliest military conflict in history in terms of total dead, with some 75 million people casualties including military and civilians, or around 3% of the world's population at the time.

- Many civilians died because of deliberate genocide, massacres, mass-bombings, disease, and starvation.

- The Soviet Union lost around 27 million people during the war, including 8.7 million military and 19 million civilians. This represents the most military deaths of any nation by a large margin.

- Germany sustained 5.3 million military losses, mostly on the Eastern Front and during the final battles in Germany.

- Of the total number of deaths in World War II, approximately 85 percent were on the Allied side and 15 percent were on the Axis side, with many of these deaths caused by war crimes committed by German and Japanese forces in occupied territories.

- Nazi Germany, as part of a deliberate program of extermination, systematically killed over 11 million people including 6 million Jews.

- In addition to Nazi concentration camps, the Soviet gulags (labor camps) led to the deaths of 3.6 million civilians.

By the grace of God, the United States and our Allies were able to defeat Germany, Japan, and the rest of the AXIS enemies. While most of the human murderers of innocents were either killed in battle or have since died, the demons involved with the AXIS forces are still with us today, working diligently to create the next World War.

We need an unprecedented level of global diplomacy and collaboration right now in order to avoid catastrophic war, and to ensure a bright future. I know that an overwhelming majority of Americans desire peace with the rest of the world. I also have no doubt that an overwhelming majority of the citizens of the nations of the world prefer peace as well. How do I know this? Because God is the source of all life, and human beings are born pure and not inherently evil.

CHAPTER 23: CONCERNS REGARDING THE COVID-19 PANDEMIC

For several months, I had the impression that I would be expected to go public about my experiences at the end of 2019, such as through the news media. However, in early November of 2019, God informed me that my time to go public would be in 2020. I asked God if there will be a clear indication of the time for when I am to go public. God responded that yes, there will be a specific major event and the time for me to go public will then be clear. God also told me that he wants humanity to "See 20/20 in 2020." In other words, God wants humanity to have clear vision, meaning a clear understanding of our situation in 2020. That situation is described in this book. In March of 2020, as I watched the COVID-19 pandemic develop, I received confirmation that the pandemic was the event that God was referring to. I was inspired to write this book and was blessed to have the time to devote to it.

Though mid-March, there was already growing concern nationwide regarding COVID-19, and new developments were reported daily. As March progressed, COVID-19 cases dramatically increased in the United States, schools nationwide were closing and transitioning to remote learning, and multiple state governments declared a state of emergency in order to mobilize resources and to request Federal Government assistance. On March 17, the Governor of Florida shut down all bars and nightclubs. On March 20, the Governor ordered all restaurants to cease indoor dining and to switch to take out and or delivery. That same day, a curfew for Orange County, Florida was issued. On March 24, the Governor issued a Stay At Home Order for Orange County, Miami-Dade County, and Alachua County

I believe that it is no coincidence that God is having me write this book now in the year 2020, while much of the world is sheltered at home, quarantined or trying to get life back to normal due to the COVID-19 global pandemic. While public figures had previously warned for years about the need for preparations for a forthcoming pandemic, so much of the world was caught unprepared, especially the United States.

As I have listened to weekly briefings, since the pandemic was recognized, I found myself learning along with the global experts in epidemiology about COVID-19, and what was true yesterday or last week is no longer true today. In other words, we are all learning together, which is disconcerting. Age groups not thought to be at risk have been recently found to be at risk, and several assumptions have been proven wrong. It is also challenging to write this chapter during a very fluid situation, when there is news daily about the pandemic and data is updated constantly

On May 13, 2020, in the article "Covid-19 infects intestines, kidneys and other organs, studies find", on www.cnn.com, it was noted that:

"The new coronavirus can infect organs throughout the body, including lungs, throat, heart, liver, brain, kidneys and the intestines, researchers reported Wednesday. Two separate reports suggest the virus goes far beyond the lungs and can attack various organs — findings that can help explain the wide range of symptoms caused by Covid-19 infection."

During the initial weeks of COVID-19 reporting in the United States, the experts and news media commented that "80 percent" of people that contract COVID-19 will only have minor symptoms and fully recover, and that children seemed to have a lower risk of contracting the virus and a lower chance of serious symptoms. In addition, people without pre-existing conditions were expected to have minimal risk of serious symptoms. All of this has been proven to be untrue. Many people without pre-existing conditions, including infants and young children have died. There is even a recently recognized condition as of a week ago, called Pediatric Multi-symptom Infectious Syndrome, which entails a young patient's immune system going into hyperdrive and causing an assortment of unusual and severe reactions, including cardiac arrest.

On Boston Children's Hospital website, Discoveries, on May 8, 2020, the following was posted in an article entitled, "COVID-19 and a serious inflammatory syndrome in children: Unpacking recent warnings":

On May 2, the International PICU-COVID-19 Collaboration,

coordinated by Jeffrey Burns, MD, MPH, chief of Critical Care Medicine at Boston Children's Hospital, convened a Zoom conference to compare notes. Pediatric experts in intensive care, cardiology, rheumatology, infectious disease, and Kawasaki disease reviewed data from several dozen cases in Europe and the U.S., offered guidance for clinicians, and laid out an agenda for research. "… there's an exponential rise in this secondary type of shock syndrome," says cardiologist Jane Newburger, MD, MPH, an international expert on Kawasaki disease who was also on the May 2 panel. "It is even possible that the antibodies that children are making to SARS-CoV2 are creating an immune reaction in the body. Nobody knows." Some children presented with some or all features seen in Kawasaki disease, an illness of children that can result in enlargement or aneurysms of the coronary arteries. Features observed included fever, rash, conjunctivitis; red, swollen hands; and red, cracked lips. Some children had clinical and laboratory signs of cytokine storm syndrome, an exaggerated systemic immune response that has caused organ damage in adults with COVID-19. Finally, many children had coagulopathies; cardiac dysfunction; diarrhea, abdominal distension, and other GI symptoms (with some children having positive stool tests for SARS-CoV-2); or acute kidney injury. Respiratory symptoms were not always a prominent feature.

Given what the medical experts know today regarding COVID-19, and the vast amount of information that we still do not know about it, one thing is clear: we need an effective vaccine before life can go back to the way it was before COVID-19. Many experts even doubt things will ever get back to the way things were before the global pandemic. As noted by USA Today on May 14, in their article, "Goodbye handshake: How do we replace the ancient greeting if coronavirus keeps us from touching?":

"I don't think we should ever shake hands ever again," Anthony Fauci, director of the National Institute of Allergy and Infectious Diseases and a leader of the White House's Coronavirus Task Force, said recently. "We've got to break that custom. Because as a matter of fact, that is really one of the major ways that you can transmit a respiratory illness." The article further went on noting, "Handshaking is a key part of Michelle Ngome's networking game as a marketing professional. Which is why Ngome, president of the African American Marketing Association and host of the "Networking With Michelle" podcast, is already missing it as social distancing rules discourage the age-old ritual."

"We didn't realize how powerful the handshake is," she said. "The handshake means connection, it means agreement, cooperation, 'hi.' It's a common courtesy." But "in the immediate future, the handshake is dead."

"And it might never come back. With the coronavirus pandemic making human touch a potentially lethal act since the virus can be transmitted with skin contact, handshaking has suddenly become socially unacceptable."

"Health experts are urging us to stay at least six feet away from people outside of our households to minimize our chances of catching COVID-19, which had infected more than 4.3 million people and killed more than 294,000 worldwide as of Wednesday afternoon. And some are saying that we should make permanent alterations to the way we physically interact with others to prevent future outbreaks, even after the coronavirus is gone. The handshake could give way to some alternative form of interaction, such as the elbow bump or the footshake."

Another consequence of COVID-19 has been the shutting down of economies all around the world for several months. Many businesses have closed that will not re-open. The U.S. economy went from only 3.5% unemployment to the highest unemployment rate since the Great Depression. Since many people have failed to be able to file for unemployment claims as websites have continuously been overloaded and crashed, and call centers are overloaded as well, there is a lag on data to reflect the actual unemployment rate. Twelve weeks since the United States safer at home orders, 44.1 million people have filed for unemployment claims as of June 12th, and that does not include undocumented workers. There have also been projections that 20%

of job positions, representing millions of jobs, will not be coming back any time soon. According to CNBC back on March 30th, Economists at the Federal Reserve's St. Louis district projected total employment reductions could reach 47 million.

Unfortunately, COVID-19 has proven to be so dangerous, due to its ease of transmission, its variable and potentially long asymptomatic period, and its lethality, that it truly will not be safe for the world to go back to pre-pandemic practices, until an effective and safe vaccine is created and distributed. While we are awaiting the creation and testing of effective and safe vaccines, most economies have already taken initial steps to reopen or have completely reopened but requesting social distancing in most cases. While this reopening is of great concern to healthcare professionals, who are already seeing a consequential increase in COVID-19 cases, the politicians responsible for each state re-opening are typically doing so by balancing the data showing the incidence of new COVID-19 cases against the increasing public protests by people suffering loss of income during the shutdown. As of June 12th, all states in the United States have relaxed or removed "Safer at Home" or "Stay at Home" orders, and economies are re-opened, even as COVID-19 infections are increasing. There is widespread concern among medical experts that we will see a sharp increase in new COVID-19 infections and deaths. I am personally surprised how many people I see that are not following the safety practices recommended by the leading medical experts, including the wearing of masks, and maintaining social distancing.

As of July 21st, COVID-19 is growing out of control in most states in the United States, and the many people that have refused to follow health official safety guidelines and have refused to wear masks and maintain social distancing are a major cause of the virus spreading. In the United States, there has been confirmation of 3,819,139 COVID-19 cases and 140,630 deaths. Globally, there has been confirmation of 14,893,706 COVID-19 cases and 615,363 deaths. There is also a consensus that the number of COVID-19 deaths reported is significantly underestimated in the United States and in other countries.

From a higher perspective, much about this COVID-19 pandemic seems unnatural to me. I am concerned that there may be a dimension of causality and evolving complications that go beyond the natural world. The COVID-19 pandemic appears to be an interdiction for the purpose of obtaining the attention of humanity. The capabilities of human intellect and modern technology have been challenged, and we have had a staggering number of deaths and many other victims suffering lasting effects. While progress is being made toward creating multiple vaccines, tests to date show that antibodies resulting from several vaccines do not last long in the bloodstream. In other words, if the antibodies do not last in the bloodstream, they probably will not protect a recipient from COVID-19 infection for the long term. However, there is hope for an effective vaccine in the first half of 2021 and the situation could be much worse.

We need to broaden our scientific research as well as include scholarly research regarding the following. I am concerned that this

COVID-19 pandemic might be another harbinger of what is known as "The Great Chastisement", which is associated with what has been called the "Third Secret of Fátima." Father Malachi Martin and at least five Popes saw this secret, which was documented in a letter. They were all extremely concerned about The Great Chastisement, which entails a series of afflictions, hardships, catastrophes, and huge loss of human life that is prophesied because humanity has sinned and failed to repent. Humanity continues to cause enormous levels of suffering and death. Our existential and many other problems are caused by our own doing. This situation is exacerbated by the increasing lack of repentance, and reduction in religious practices. Those people that turn away from God find that God is willing to allow them to live life without God active in it. As God pulls back, it leaves these people vulnerable to attacks from the Forces of Evil.

In order to understand the Third Secret of Fátima, we need to take a more detailed look at all of the information that was shared at Fátima. As mentioned in Chapter 5, the Catholic Church performed due diligence and has validated all apparitions, prophesies, and the miracle that occurred at Fátima, Portugal, in 1917. Sister Lúcia wrote that Our Lady shared one secret that had three parts. What many people call Third Secret of Fátima is actually the third part of the secret. For context, it will be beneficial to review all three parts of the secret.

In her book, *Fátima in Sister Lúcia's own words*, (Lúcia, July 2007, 16th edition, Kondor), Sister Lúcia describes the first two parts of the secret shared by the Blessed Virgin Mary on July 13, 2017, and these prophesy the end of World War One, the forthcoming World War Two, the Cold War spread of communism and Russian aggression, and the assassination attempt on Saint John Paul II. It also includes a strong recommendation for devotion to the Immaculate Heart of Mary.

"Well, the secret is made up of three distinct parts, two of which I am now going to reveal. The first part is the vision of hell. Our Lady showed us a great sea of fire which seemed to be under the earth. Plunged in this fire were demons and souls in human form, like transparent burning embers, all blackened or burnished bronze, floating about in the conflagration, now raised into the air by the flames that issued from within themselves together with great clouds of smoke, now falling back on every side like sparks in a huge fire, without weight or equilibrium, and amid shrieks and groans of pain and despair, which horrified us and made us tremble with fear. The demons could be distinguished by their terrifying and repellent likeness to frightful and unknown animals, all black and transparent. This vision lasted but an instant. How can we ever be grateful enough to our kind heavenly Mother, who had already prepared us by promising, in the first Apparition, to take us to Heaven. Otherwise, I think we would have died of fear and terror.

We then looked up at Our Lady, who said to us so kindly and so sadly: "You have seen hell where the souls of poor sinners go. To save them, God wishes to establish in the world devotion to my Immaculate Heart. If what I say to you is done, many souls will be saved and there will be peace. The war is going to end, but if people do not cease offending God, a worse one will break out. When you see a night illumined by an unknown light, know that this is the great sign given you by God that He is about to punish the world for its crimes, by means of war, famine, and persecutions of the Church and of the Holy Father. "To prevent this, I shall come to ask for the consecration of Russia to my Immaculate Heart, and the Communion of reparation on the First Saturdays. If my requests are heeded, Russia will be converted, and there will be peace; if not, she will spread her errors throughout the world, causing wars and persecutions of the Church. The good will be martyred; the Holy Father will have much to suffer; various nations will be annihilated.

In the end, my Immaculate Heart will triumph. The Holy Father will consecrate Russia to me, and she will be converted, and a period of peace will be granted to the world."

Sister Lúcia declared that the third part of the secret was not to be made public until 1960, saying that, "by that time, it will be more clearly understood", and, "because the Blessed Virgin wishes it so." However, when 1960 arrived, the Vatican declined to publish it and published an official press release saying that the secret would remain under seal. This announcement generated widespread speculation. According to the *New York Times*, speculation over the content of the secret ranged from "worldwide nuclear annihilation" to "deep rifts in the Roman Catholic Church that lead to rival papacies."

The third part of the secret was written by Sister Lúcia on January 3, 1944. This is what the Vatican published on June 26, 2000:

"J.M.J.

The third part of the secret revealed at the Cova da Iria-Fátima, on 13 July 1917.

I write in obedience to you, my God, who command me to do so, through his Excellency the Bishop of Leiria and through your Most Holy Mother and mine.

After the two parts which I have already explained, at the left of Our Lady and a little above, we saw an Angel with a flaming sword in his left hand; flashing, it gave out flames that looked as though they would set the world on fire; but they died out in contact with the splendour that Our Lady radiated towards him from her right hand: pointing to the earth with his right hand, the Angel cried out in a loud voice: 'Penance, Penance, Penance!' And we saw in an immense light that is God: 'something similar to how people appear in a mirror when they pass in front of it' a Bishop dressed in White, 'we had the impression that it was the Holy Father'. Other Bishops, Priests, men, and women Religious going up a steep mountain, at the top of which there was a big Cross of rough-hewn trunks as of a cork-tree with the bark; before reaching there the Holy

Father passed through a big city half in ruins and half trembling with halting step, afflicted with pain and sorrow, he prayed for the souls of the corpses he met on his way; having reached the top of the mountain, on his knees at the foot of the big Cross he was killed by a group of soldiers who fired bullets and arrows at him, and in the same way there died one after another the other Bishops, Priests, men and women Religious, and various lay people of different ranks and positions. Beneath the two arms of the Cross

there were two Angels each with a crystal aspersorium in his hand, in which they gathered up the blood of the Martyrs and with it sprinkled the souls that were making their way to God.

Tuy-3-1-1944".

There has been controversy regarding the above letter. Several writers claim that the official Vatican release is different from the letter written by Sister Lúcia. Some say a page is missing that covers the Apocalypse and the apostasy of the Catholic Church. Some say that the official release has more pages but is missing content from Sister Lúcia's letter.

As reported by Phoebe Natanson for ABC News on May 14, 2010, during his visit to the Shrine of Our Lady of Fátima, Pope Benedict XVI told reporters that the Third Secret did not only refer to the attempted assassination of Pope John Paul II in Saint Peter's Square in 1981, but that it "has a permanent and ongoing significance." He said, "its significance could even be extended to include the suffering the Church is going through today as a result of the recent reports of sexual abuse involving the clergy."

This is mentioned in the English translation from Daniel J. Lynch, *The Call to Total Consecration to the Immaculate Heart of Mary* (Lynch, 1991):

In a 1980 interview for the German magazine Stimme des Glaubens published in October 1981, Pope John Paul II was asked explicitly to speak about the Third Secret. He said:

"Because of the seriousness of its contents, in order not to encourage the worldwide power of Communism to carry out certain coups, my predecessors in the chair of Peter have diplomatically preferred to withhold its publication. On the other hand, it should be sufficient for all Christians to know this much: if there is a message in which it is said that the oceans will flood entire sections of the earth; that, from one moment to the other, millions of people will perish... there is no longer any point in really wanting to publish this secret message. Many want to know merely out of curiosity, or because of their taste for sensationalism, but they forget that 'to know' implies for them a responsibility. It is dangerous to want to satisfy one's curiosity only, if one is convinced that we can do nothing against a catastrophe that has been predicted." He held up his rosary and stated, "Here is the remedy against this evil. Pray, pray, and ask for nothing else. Put everything in the hands of the Mother of God." Asked what would happen in the Church, he said: "We must be prepared to undergo great trials in the not-too-distant future; trials that will require us to be ready to give up even our lives, and a total gift of self to Christ and for Christ. Through your prayers and mine, it is possible to alleviate this tribulation, but it is no longer possible to avert it, because it is only in this way that the Church can be effectively renewed. How many times, indeed, has the renewal of the Church been affected in blood? This time, again, it will not be otherwise. We must be strong, ... we must entrust ourselves to Christ and to His holy Mother, and we must be attentive, very attentive, to the prayer of the Rosary."

According to Frere Michel de la Sainte Trinite, *The Whole Truth About Fátima, Volume III* (Frere Michel de la Sainte Trinite, 1990), when Lúcia was asked about the Third Secret, she said it was "in the Gospels and in the Apocalypse", and at one point she had even specified Apocalypse chapters 8 to 13, a range that includes the Book of Revelation 12:4, the chapter and verse cited by Pope John Paul II in his homily in Fátima on 13 May 2000.

Before he passed away, Father Malachi Martin mentioned that there were several indications that The Great Chastisement was coming in the foreseeable future. He specified one indicator being an increase in the number of cases of demonic possession of young children, under the age of eight years old, through no fault of their own, and not due to anything intentional that the parents did. Father Martin saw this phenomenon as punishment of parents. Father Martin claimed that the accident that ultimately caused his death was due to his attempting to exorcise a four-year-old girl, and Satan retaliating by causing him to take a devastating fall at his home. He stated that he had climbed up a ladder in his library to obtain a book, and even though nobody else was with him in his apartment, something grabbed him above the ankles and threw him down. He was able to call a close friend for help and told him what had happened, and that "Old Scratch", meaning Satan, was not happy with his attempts to help the possessed girl. Soon afterwards, Father Martin lapsed into a coma and passed away. This event is described in the film, *Hostage To The Devil*, 2016, which was directed by Marty Stalker.

On the same theme as The Great Chastisement, it is worth mentioning that another Catholic Church-validated Marian vision occurred more recently at Akita, Japan on October 13, 1973. As recounted by John Ata at https://www.ewtn.com/catholicism/library/message-from-our-lady—akita-japan-5167, the Blessed Virgin Mary appeared to Sister Agnes Sasagawa and stated:

> "My dear daughter, listen well to what I have to say to you. You will inform your superior."

> After a short silence: "As I told you, if men do not repent and better themselves, the Father will inflict a terrible punishment on all humanity. It will be a punishment greater than the

deluge, such as one will never see before. Fire will fall from the sky and will wipe out a great part of humanity, the good as well as the bad, sparing neither priests nor faithful. The survivors will find themselves so desolate that they will envy the dead. The only arms which will remain for you will be the Rosary and the Sign left by My Son. Each day recite the prayers of the Rosary. With the Rosary, pray for the Pope, the bishops, and priests."

"The work of the devil will infiltrate even into the Church in such a way that one will see cardinals opposing cardinals, bishops against bishops. The priests who venerate me will be scorned and opposed by their confreres...churches and altars sacked; the Church will be full of those who accept compromises and the demon will press many priests and consecrated souls to leave the service of the Lord. The demon will be especially implacable against souls consecrated to God. The thought of the loss of so many souls is the cause of my sadness. If sins increase in number and gravity, there will be no longer pardon for them."

"With courage, speak to your superior. He will know how to encourage each one of you to pray and to accomplish works of reparation. It is Bishop Ito, who directs your community."

And She smiled and then said: "You have still something to ask? Today is the last time that I will speak to you in living voice. From now on you will obey the one sent to you and your superior. Pray very much the prayers of the Rosary. I alone am able still to save you from the calamities which approach. Those who place their confidence in me will be saved."

This is a wakeup call for all of humanity that we need to take immediate actions to address the dangers that we face. We will be much more effective and efficient if we all work together toward common beneficial goals. We are all connected, and we all need to be prepared to help each other. The COVID-19 pandemic has shown us that all of humanity is connected from a health and wellness perspective. The financial crisis of 2008 taught us that our global financial infrastructure is highly connected, intertwined, and complex. We are connected in so many ways and our future depends upon us eliminating conflict and working together. Considering the consistency of Marian prophecies that we have received, I also believe that prayer and repentance is important for everyone.

CHAPTER 24: A CALL TO ACTION

The following is a call to action for every human being:

To Everyone:

- Be respectful & protective of family, friends, neighbors, community, emergency services personnel, and other people as well.

- Every day, dedicate meaningful prayer time to the God of all creation, reflect upon your blessings, give thanks to God, repent for any wrongdoings, pray for those you care about, and pray for things that you desire. Develop and strengthen your faith and know you are not alone.

- Strive to be the best that you can be every day in your words and in your actions.

- Help others and work together to solve problems and improve the quality of life for all.

To all Parents:

- Ensure that your children know that they are loved and special.

- Teach them that life is sacred, the importance of faith, the dangers in our world, to treat other people with respect and courtesy, to help others when they are able, and the importance of lifelong learning and continuous improvement.

- Encourage your children to have a vision for their lives, to pursue the dreams of their heart, and to achieve important goals.

To all Leaders of Nations and Military Forces:

- De-escalate tensions between nations and work together to protect humanity.

To all Professionals that fight evil, including clergy, demonologists, physicians, psychologists, law enforcement personnel, intelligence agency personnel, military personnel, and researchers:

- Study the topics covered in this book in order to protect yourselves and to be better able to discern when preternatural activity is affecting any given situation.

- Increase and or support scientific research and share findings and best practices.

- Implement modern information technology for communications, collaboration, and easy to use knowledge base functionality.

- Establish online resources optimized for different types of professionals.

- Implement helpful and practical online resources for the public.

- Establish a governance framework incorporating regulatory compliance, with an effective and standardized approach to logging requests for help, identifying and assigning optimal resources, providing discernment and diagnosis, delivery of care, and documenting both the approach and resolution.

- We can only manage and control what we measure and analyze.

- Plan, prepare, and execute nationwide and international collaboration toward common goals.

CHAPTER 25: CONCLUDING REMARKS

While some people are blessed to learn of God's calling for them early in life, it was not until I was over fifty years old that God revealed his mission for me. Mine is a mission of education and of spreading peace and faith. I am grateful and honored that God has chosen me to help share vital information to facilitate bringing humanity together to make our world a safer and better place. I understand why he waited as long as he did to inform me, since my life experiences provide evidence and lessons learned that will help many other people. Through the information that God has me share, God intends to level the playing field for humanity, and to provide humanity with a better chance of overcoming the Forces of Evil, because good people are needlessly dying every day and millions more are suffering because of attacks by the Forces of Evil.

Too many people are preoccupied with materialism, modernism, science, and technology; and foregoing faith, they do not realize that science and faith are both aspects of the same reality that we experience. In other words, as people have ignored or turned away from God, it has made them, and all of us, more vulnerable to the Forces of Evil. Even many people who practice religion do not understand the source of demonic attacks and afflictions, because they have not received religious education covering demons. This is also true for clergy of several faiths.

While there are many exorcists that say we should not "look under every rock" for demons as the causes of all of our problems, and there is validity to this statement, I solemnly assure you that the increasing risk of nuclear war, genocides, heinous crimes, the rise of and aggressions of hate groups, and the majority of the most deplorable human transgressions are the deliberate result of the efforts of Satan and the Forces of Evil to manipulate human beings. We can overcome these challenges by strengthening our faith and working together.

Please do not be distracted by the forthcoming critics of this book. I am sure that you will find that their objections and views will be based upon any of the following potential reasons: their ego preferring them to be in the spotlight, their lack of belief in God, their lack of understanding of God's power and ways, their lack of believing that modern day messengers of God can exist, and possibly their alignment with Satan to facilitate disregarding any proof of the reality of Satan and the Forces of Evil. I heartily welcome amicable discussions regarding facts, anything that helps us to improve human relations and to be more effective in combatting evil, and anything that helps us to resolve the problems faced by humanity.

I am encouraging a logical and scientific approach. It is my hope that this book will inspire productive discussions and collaborative actions that change our world. By reducing human conflict, encouraging each of us to be respectful and protective of each other, strengthening families, strengthening communities, alleviating social rifts, educating humanity against the dangers of fake news, inspiring increased political cooperation, and expediting international collaboration, we can make our world a safer and better place!

I am reminded of this Holy Scripture:

Do not be conformed to this world, but

be transformed by the renewing of your

minds, so that you may discern what

is the will of God — what is good and

acceptable and perfect.

Romans 12:2 (NRSV-CE)

I have found the following books, listed by category and by author in alphabetical order, to be extremely informative. Several have already been mentioned in this book.

Books covering the reality of God and Satan and the Battle of Good Versus Evil:

Amorth, G. (1999). *An Exorcist Tells His Story*. Ignatius Press.

Amorth, G. (2000). *An Exorcist More Stories*. Ignatius.

Amorth, G. (2016). *An Exorcist Explains the Demonic: The Antics of Satan and His Army of Fallen Angels.* Sophia Institute Press.

Baglio, M. (2009). *The Rite: The Making of a Modern Exorcist.* Doubleday Religion.

Brittle, G. (2013). *The Demonologist: The Extraordinary Career of Ed and Lorraine Warren.* Graymalkin Media.

Fortea, J.A. (2006). *Interview With An Exorcist*, Ascension Press.

Gallagher, R. (2020). *Demonic Foes: My Twenty-Five Years as a Psychiatrist Investigating Possessions, Diabolic Attacks, and the Paranormal.* HarperCollins Publishers.

Larson, B. (1999). *Larson's Book of Spiritual Warfare* Paperback. Thomas Nelson Publishers.

Martin, M. (1992). *Hostage to the Devil: The Possession and Exorcism of Five Contemporary Americans.* HarperCollins.

Peck, M.S. (2009). *Glimpses of the Devil: A Psychiatrist's Personal Accounts of Possession.* Free Press.

Ryave, J.L. (2020). *New Proof of God & Satan.* Bring Humanity Together, LLC.

Sarchie, R. & Cool, L. *Deliver Us From Evil*. St. Martin's Paperbacks.

Thigpen, P. (2015). *Saints Who Battled Satan: Seventeen Holy Warriors Who Can Teach You How to Fight the Good Fight and Vanquish Your Ancient Enemy*. Tan Books.

Books with helpful prayers:

Ripperger, C. (2020). *Deliverance Prayers For Use By The Laity*. Sensus Traditionis Press.

Ryave, J.L. (2020). New Proof of God & Satan. Bring Humanity Together, LLC.

Thigpen, P. (2014). *Manual of Spiritual Warfare*. Tan Books.

U.S. Conference of Catholic Bishops (2021). *Prayers to Protect Us*. USCCB.

Wilson, L. (2021). *Essential Spiritual Warfare Prayers for Protection and Deliverance*. Pauline Books & Media.

Wilson, L. (2021). *Essential Healing Prayers for Peace and Strength*. Pauline Books & Media.

Books attesting to the immortality of the soul:

Alexander III, E. (2012). *Proof of Heaven: A Neurosurgeon's Journey into the Afterlife*. Simon & Schuster Paperbacks.

Burpo, T. & Vincent, L. (2014). *Heaven is for Real: A Little Boy's Astounding Story of His Trip to Heaven and Back*. Thomas Nelson.

Kübler-Ross, E. (1991). *On Life After Death*. Celestial Arts.

Moody, Jr., R. (2015). *Life After Life*. HarperSanFrancisco

Ryave, J.L. (2020). *New Proof of God & Satan*. Bring Humanity Together, LLC.

Tucker, J. (2013). *Return to Life: Extraordinary cases of Children Who Remember Past Lives*. St. Martin's Press.

Van Den Aardweg, G. (2009). *Hungry Souls: Supernatural Visits, Messages, and Warnings from Purgatory*. Tan Books.

Books with enlightening content:

Rotbart, H. (2016). *Miracles We Have Seen*. Health Communications, Inc.

Heiser, M. S. (2019). *The Unseen Realm: Recovering the Supernatural Worldview of the Bible*, Lexham Press

Heiser, M. S. (2020). *Demons*, Lexham Press

Laszewski, W. (2021). *The World of Marian Apparitions: Mary's Appearances and Messages from Fatima to Today*. Sophia Institute Press

Informative documentaries:

Hostage to the Devil, Director Marty Stalker, 2016, Documentary

Return of the Exorcists, Director Declan McCormack, 2015, Documentary

The Devil & Father Amorth, Director William Friedkin, 2017, Documentary

The Sons of Sam: A Descent Into Darkness, Director Joshua Zeman, 2021, Documentary

Films with relevant themes:

Deliver Us From Evil, Director Scott Derrickson, 2014

Nefarious, Directors Chuck Konzelman and Cary Solomon, 2023

The Rite, Director Mikael Håfström, 2011

You do not need any special capabilities to change the world for the better. Each of us is important and can change our world simply by modeling good character and setting an example for those around us. You are blessed with the gift of life and unique attributes and talents directly from God. You are the only human being out of 7.8 billion human beings on Earth that is exactly like you. That should make you feel special, and God sees you as special.

I hope that this book has been a blessing to you. For more information, important resources, videos, and to support the spreading of peace and faith, please visit www.bringhumanitytogether.com. Peace be with you.

ACKNOWLEDGEMENTS

I would like to express my deep appreciation to Father Gary Thomas, who provided the Foreword to this book, and also provided me with valuable guidance and a wealth of information, which has been derived from his extensive professional experience and insights as a Priest, Exorcist, and Pastor. Father Gary is an excellent leader and is a role model for many people in terms of moral excellence, understanding of Roman Catholic doctrines, exemplification of a healthy spiritual life, and devotion to serving humanity. Father Gary is also a great teacher and speaker, who is passionate, knowledgeable, and extraordinarily articulate.

I would also like to express my gratitude to the Chancellor for Canonical Affairs and Vicar General as well as the Exorcist for the Diocese of Orlando. Both of them were generous with their time and I learned a lot from my meetings with them. Out of respect for their privacy, I have not mentioned their names.

ABOUT THE AUTHOR

James L. Ryave has a background of over thirty years of business and information technology consulting, providing thought leadership and industry best practices. He is also a religious demonologist with deep knowledge of Holy Scriptures, has extensive experience researching paranormal phenomena, and is a teacher of best practices in these areas. He is a passionate advocate for helping others, providing community service, and giving back to society. His mission is Bring Humanity Together and the website is www.bringhumanitytogether.com .

APPENDIX A: HELPFUL PRAYERS

Christianity

Prayer to Saint Michael the Archangel

Saint Michael the Archangel,
defend us in battle,
be our protector against the wickedness and snares of the devil;
may God rebuke him, we humbly pray;
and do thou, O Prince of the Heavenly Host,
by the power of God,
thrust into hell Satan and all the evil spirits who prowl about the
world seeking the ruin of souls.
Amen.

Prayer against Malefice

Kyrie Eleison.
God, our Lord, King of ages.
All-powerful and All-mighty,
you who made everything and who transform
everything simply by your will.
You who in Babylon changed into dew
the flames of the "seven times hotter" furnace
and protected and saved the three holy children.
You are the doctor and the physician of our soul.
You are the salvation of those who turn to you.
We beseech you to make powerless,
banish and drive out every diabolic power,
presence and machination;
every evil influence, malefice or evil eye
and all evil actions aimed against your servant (*name*).
Where there is envy and malice, give us an
abundance of goodness, endurance, victory,
and charity.
O'Lord, you who love man, we beg you to reach
out your powerful hands and your most high and mighty
arms and come to our aid.
Help us, who are made in your image;
send the angel of peace over us,
to protect us body and soul.
May he keep at bay and vanquish every evil power,
every poison or malice invoked against us

by corrupt and envious people.

Then, under the protection of your authority may

we sing, in gratitude,

"The Lord is my salvation; whom should I fear?

I will not fear evil because you are with me,

my God, my strength, my powerful Lord,

Lord of peace and Father of all ages."

Yes, Lord our God, be merciful to us, your image,

and save your servant (*name*) from every threat or harm;

from the evil one, and protect (*him/her*)

by raising (*him/her*) above all evil.

We ask you this through the intercession

of our Most Blessed, Glorious Lady,

Mary ever Virgin, Mother of God,

of the most splendid Archangels

and All your Saints.

Amen!

Prayer against Every Evil

Spirit of our God, Father, Son, and Holy Spirit,

Most Holy Trinity, Immaculate Virgin Mary,

Angels, Archangels, and Saints of Heaven, descend

upon me.

Please purify me, Lord, mold me,

fill me with yourself and use me.

Banish all the Forces of Evil from me,

destroy them, vanquish them,

so that I can be healthy and do good deeds.

Banish from me all spells, witchcraft, black magic,

malefice, ties, maledictions, and the evil eye;

diabolic infestations, oppressions, possessions;

all that is evil and sinful,

jealousy, perfidy, envy;

physical, psychological, moral,

spiritual, diabolical ailments.

Burn all these evils in hell,

that they may never again touch me

or any other creature in the entire world.

I command and bid all the powers

who molest me – by the power of God all powerful,

in the name of Jesus Christ our Savior;

through the intercession

of the Immaculate Virgin Mary – to leave me forever,

and to be consigned into the everlasting hell,

where they will be bound by Saint Michael

the Archangel, Saint Gabriel, Saint Raphael,

and our Guardian Angels,

and where they will be crushed

under the heel of the Immaculate Virgin Mary.

Prayer for Deliverance #1

My Lord, you are all powerful,

you are God, you are Father.

We beg you through the intercession and help

of the Archangels Michael, Raphael, and Gabriel
for the deliverance of our brothers and sisters
who are enslaved by the evil one.
All saints of Heaven, come to our aid.

From anxiety, sadness, and obsessions,
We beg you, Free us, O Lord.
From hatred, fornication, and envy,
We beg you, Free us, O Lord.
From thoughts of jealousy, rage, and death,
We beg you, Free us, O Lord.
From every thought of suicide and abortion,
We beg you, Free us, O Lord.
From every form of sinful sexuality,
We beg you, Free us, O Lord.
From every division in our family,
and every harmful friendship,
We beg you, Free us, O Lord.
From every sort of spell, malefice, and witchcraft,
and every form of the occult,
We beg you, Free us, O Lord.

Lord, you who said,
"I leave you peace, my peace I give you",
grant that, through the intercession
of the Virgin Mary, we may be liberated
from every evil spell and enjoy your peace always.

In the name of Christ, our Lord.
Amen.

Prayer for Deliverance #2

O Jesus our Savior,
my Lord and my God,
my God and my all.
With Your sacrifice of the Cross,
You redeemed us and defeated the power of Satan.
I beg You to deliver me from every evil presence
and every evil influence.
I ask You in Your name,
I ask you for the sake of Your Wounds,
I ask you for the sake of Your Blood,
I ask you for the sake of Your Cross,
I ask you through the intercession of Mary,
Immaculate and sorrowful.

May the blood and water that flow from Your side
wash over me to purify me, deliver me, and heal me.
Amen.

Prayer for Protection

Lord Jesus Christ,
in your love and mercy,
establish a perimeter of protection around myself

and all my loved ones, those who pray for us,
and their loved ones as well.

May the Holy Angels guard me and all my possessions,
establishing a perimeter of protection around me rendering
me immune from any kind of demonic influence.

I ask that no demonic bondage, door, demonic entity, portal, astral
projection or disembodied spirit may enter the space 100 yards in all
directions of me.
I ask that any demons within this vicinity be rendered deaf, dumb,
and blind; that You would strip them of all weapons, armor, power,
illusions, and authority;
that You would bind, rebuke, and disable them from
communicating or interacting with each other in any way.
Remove them, O Lord, and send them directly to the foot of Your
Cross. O Jesus, Son of the Most High, I ask this in
Your Glorious and Most Holy Name. Amen.

Anime Christi

Soul of Christ, sanctify me;
Body of Christ, save me;
Blood of Christ, inebriate me;
Water from the side of Christ, wash me;
Passion of Christ, strengthen me;
O good Jesus, hear me;
Within your wounds, hide me;

Let me never be separated from you;

From the evil one, protect me;

At the hour of my death, call me;

And bid me come to you; that with your saints;

I may praise you forever and ever.

Amen.

Breathe on me

Breath on me, Breath of God,
fill me with life anew,
that I may love what thou dost love,
and I do what thou wouldst do.

Breath on me, Breath of God,
until my heart is pure,
until my will is one with thine,
to do and to endure.

Breath on me, Breath of God,
til I am wholly thine,
until this earthly part of me
glows with thy fire divine.

Breath on me, Breath of God,
so shall I never die;
but live with thee the perfect life
of thine eternity.

Judaism

Psalms, Chapter 91: Assurance of God's Protection

He who dwells in the covert of the Most High will lodge in the shadow of the Almighty.

I shall say of the Lord [that He is] my shelter and my fortress, my God in Whom I trust.

For He will save you from the snare that traps from the devastating pestilence.

With His wing He will cover you, and under His wings you will take refuge; His truth is an encompassing shield.

You will not fear the fright of night, the arrow that flies by day;

Pestilence that prowls in darkness, destruction that ravages at noon.

A thousand will be stationed at your side, and ten thousand at your right hand; but it will not approach you.

You will but gaze with your eyes, and you will see the annihilation of the wicked.

For you [said], "The Lord is my refuge"; the Most High you made your dwelling.

No harm will befall you, nor will a plague draw near to your tent.

For He will command His angels on your behalf to guard you in all your ways.

On [their] hands they will bear you, lest your foot stumble on a stone.

On a young lion and a cobra you will tread; you will trample the young lion and the serpent.

For he yearns for Me, and I shall rescue him; I shall fortify him because he knows My name.

He will call Me and I shall answer him; I am with him in distress; I shall rescue him and I shall honor him.

With length of days I shall satiate him, and I shall show him My salvation.

Psalms, Chapter 20: Prayer for Victory

For the conductor, a song of David.

May the Lord answer you on a day of distress; may the name of the God of Jacob fortify you.

May He send your aid from His sanctuary, and may He support you from Zion.

May He remember all your meal offerings and may He accept your fat burnt offerings forever.

May He give you as your heart [desires], and may He fulfill all your counsel.

Let us sing praises for your salvation, and let us assemble in the name of our God; may the Lord fulfill all your requests.

Now I know that the Lord saved His anointed; He answered him from His holy heavens; with the mighty acts of salvation from His right hand.

These trust in chariots and these in horses, but we-we mention the name of the Lord our God.

They kneel and fall, but we rise and gain strength.

Lord, save [us]; may the King answer us on the day we call.

Psalms, Chapter 90: God's Eternity and Human Frailty

A prayer of Moses, the man of God.

O Lord, You have been our dwelling place throughout all generations.
Before the mountains were born, and You brought forth the earth and the inhabited world, and from everlasting to everlasting, You are God.
You bring man to the crushing point, and You say, "Return, O sons of men."
For a thousand years are in Your eyes like yesterday, which passed, and a watch in the night.
You carry them away as a flood; they are like a sleep; in the morning, like grass it passes away.

In the morning, it blossoms and passes away; in the evening, it is cut off and withers.

For we perish from Your wrath, and from Your anger we are dismayed.

You have placed our iniquities before You, [the sins of] our youth before the light of Your countenance.

For all our days have passed away in Your anger; we have consumed our years as a murmur.

The days of our years because of them are seventy years, and if with increase, eighty years; but their pride is toil and pain, for it passes quickly and we fly away.

Who knows the might of Your wrath, and according to Your fear is Your anger.

So teach the number of our days, so that we shall acquire a heart of wisdom.

Return, O Lord, how long? And repent about Your servants.

Satiate us in the morning with Your loving-kindness, and let us sing praises and rejoice with all our days.

Cause us to rejoice according to the days that You afflicted us, the years that we saw evil.

May Your works appear to Your servants, and Your beauty to their sons.

And may the pleasantness of the Lord our God be upon us, and the work of our hands establish for us, and the work of our hands establish it.

Psalms, Chapter 140: Prayer for Deliverance from Enemies

For the conductor, a song of David.
Rescue me, O Lord, from an evil man from a man of robbery You shall guard me.

Who plotted evil things in their heart; every day they gather to wage war.

They whetted their tongue like a serpent; the venom of a spider is under their lips forever.

Guard me, O Lord, from the hands of a wicked man; from a man of robbery You shall watch me, who plotted to cause my steps to slip.

Haughty men have concealed a snare for me, and [with] ropes they spread a net beside [my] path; they laid traps for me constantly.

I said to the Lord, "You are my God." Hearken, O Lord, to the voice of my supplications.

God, O Lord, the might of my salvation; You shall protect my head on the day of battle.

O Lord, do not grant the desires of the wicked; do not let his thoughts succeed, for they are constantly haughty.

The numbers of those who surround me, may the lies of their lips cover them.

Let fiery coals descend on them; He will cast them into fire, in wars, so that they will not rise.

A slanderer will not be established on earth; a man of violence, the evil will trap him with thrust upon thrust.

I know that the Lord will perform the judgment of a poor man, the cause of the needy.

But the righteous will thank Your name; the upright will sit before You.

Psalms, Chapter 23: The Divine Shepherd

A song of David.
The Lord is my shepherd; I shall not want.
He causes me to lie down in green pastures; He leads me beside still waters.
He restores my soul; He leads me in paths of righteousness for His name's sake.
Even when I walk in the valley of darkness, I will fear no evil for You are with me; Your rod and Your staff-they comfort me.
You set a table before me in the presence of my adversaries; You anointed my head with oil; my cup overflows.
May only goodness and kindness pursue me all the days of my life, and I will dwell in the house of the Lord for length of days.

Psalms, Chapter 1: The Two Ways

The praises of a man are that he did not follow the counsel of the wicked, neither did he stand in the way of sinners nor sit in the company of scorners.

But his desire is in the law of the Lord, and in His law he meditates day and night.

He shall be as a tree planted beside rivulets of water, which brings forth its fruit in its season, and its leaves do not wilt; and whatever he does prospers.

Not so the wicked, but [they are] like chaff that the wind drives away.

Therefore, the wicked shall not stand up in judgment, nor shall the sinners in the congregation of the righteous.

For the Lord knows the way of the righteous, but the way of the wicked shall perish.

The Shema (Deuteronomy 6:4 – 6:9)

Hear, O Israel, Adonai, our God, Adonai, is One.

Blessed be the name of his glorious majesty forever and ever.

You shall love Adonai your God with all your heart, with all your soul, and with all your might. And these words which I command you today shall be in your heart. You shall teach them diligently to your children, and you shall speak of them when you are sitting at home and when you go on a journey, when you lie down and when you rise up. You shall bind them as a sign on your hand, and they shall be frontlets between your eyes. You shall inscribe them on the doorposts of your house and on your gates.

Blessing for the Home (Birkat HaBayit)

Let no sorrow come through this gate.
Let no trouble come in this dwelling.
Let no fright come through this door.
Let no conflict come to this department.
Let there be blessing and peace in this place.

A Prayer at Bedtime

Praised are You, Adonai, our God, Ruler of the universe, who closes my eyes in sleep, my eyelids in slumber.
May it be Your will, Adonai, My God and the God of my ancestors, to lie me down in peace and then to raise me up in peace.
Let no disturbing thoughts upset me, no evil dreams nor troubling fantasies.
May my bed be complete and whole in Your sight.
Grant me light so that I do not sleep the sleep of death, for it is You who illumines and enlightens.
Praised are You, Adonai, whose majesty gives light to the universe.

Special Prayer for Protection at Night

In the name of Adonai the God of Israel:
May the angel Michael be at my right,
and the angel Gabriel be at my left;
and in front of me the angel Uriel,
and behind me the angel Raphael...
and above my head the *Sh'khinah* (Divine Presence).

APPENDIX B: RESOURCES IN THE UNITED STATES FOR THOSE SUFFERING

The helpful resources on the following pages are for anyone that is suffering. The Forces of Evil can have a significant influence on human beings and the negative circumstances for each of the categories listed. Please keep in mind that God has a purpose for your life and even if it has not yet been revealed to you, tomorrow can be a better day than today. Never underestimate the power and benefits of prayer. Furthermore, you are never truly alone, because there are many people that are available and eager to help you.

The information that follows was sourced on the internet and accurate at the time it was listed but may change over time. The author and publisher are not responsible for the current accuracy of the following information, which is listed by title in alphabetical order.

1. Prevent Child Abuse

2. Prevent Cruelty to Animals

3. Prevent Domestic Violence

4. Prevent Human Trafficking

5. Prevent Substance Abuse

6. Prevent Suicide

7. Seek Mental Healthcare

PREVENT CHILD ABUSE

Child abuse is illegal and should not be tolerated. If you believe that a child is being abused and in danger, do not hesitate and call your local law enforcement immediately. For most locations in the United States, you can **dial 9-1-1**.

The following resources were sourced from the Prevent Child Abuse America website: https://preventchildabuse.org/resources/

Hotlines, Crisis, and Support contacts for child abuse

Childhelp: 800-4-A-CHILD

Operates 24 hours a day, seven days a week. Call or text the hotline for crisis intervention, information, literature, and referrals.

National Center for Missing & Exploited Children: 800-THE-LOST (843-5678)

24-hour Hotline and CyberTipline (for reporting child sexual exploitation).
If you think you have seen a missing child, contact the National Center for Missing & Exploited Children 24-hours a day, 7 days a week. The Congress-authorized Cybertipline is a means for reporting crimes against children. Reports may

be made 24-hours a day, 7 days a week, online at www.cybertipline.com.

National Runaway Safeline: Help for Runaway and Homeless Youth: 800-786-2929

National Runaway Safeline is a 24/7 hotline that serves as the national communication system for runaway and homeless youth (RHY) providing crisis intervention, information and referrals, and other resources. The RHY hotline can be reached:

- By phone: 1-800-RUNAWAY / 1-800-786-2929
- By email: https://www.1800runaway.org/crisis-online-services/
- Online chat: https://www.1800runaway.org/ and select "Chat Now"

Parent Resources

Prevent Child Abuse America®: 800-CHILDREN (244-5373)

A resource for tips, referrals, and parenting materials. In participating states, calls will be connected to the state chapter. For non-participating states, the national office.

Healthy Families America®: 312-663-3520

An innovative initiative designed to support and educate new parents through voluntary home visitation.

National Children's Advocacy Center: 256-533-KIDS (5437)

The National Children's Advocacy Center is a non-profit organization that provides training, prevention, and treatment services to fight child abuse and neglect.

Circle of Parents: 804-308-0841

A family support program offering free weekly meetings for anyone in a parenting role wanting to discuss issues related to raising children.

Family Resources

Grandparent Information Center

800-424-3410
For grandparents raising grandchildren, professionals, support groups, researchers, and policy makers to discuss issues related to raising children.

Preventing Child Abuse & Neglect

The Child Welfare Information Gateway is a service of the Children's Bureau, the Administration for Children and Families, and the U.S. Department of Health and Human Services. The following is helpful information from their website: https://www.childwelfare.gov/topics/preventing/

The 2018 Family First Prevention Services Act requires the child welfare field to continue building on its knowledge and implementation of evidence-informed prevention practices to help mitigate and end the devastating consequences of child abuse and neglect. Due to the long-term effects child abuse and neglect can have on a child's physical, psychological, and behavioral health, providing quality primary prevention programs and services is vital. Programs and services that focus on the overall health and well-being of both children and families and that are designed to promote resiliency and parent capacity are key to preventing child maltreatment. To increase the likelihood that children are safe from maltreatment, communities should move beyond efforts solely built on public awareness campaigns to an approach that emphasizes the vital role of community, early intervention services, and collaboration and acknowledges that all parents need support.

The resources listed below are accessible on the website and offer information on decreasing the risk of maltreatment and supporting and strengthening families, including protective factors, public awareness, community activities, positive parenting, prevention programs, and more. You can also find additional information on the National Child Abuse Prevention Month website.

Overview

Understanding child abuse prevention and what to do when children are at risk. Includes frequently asked questions and links to related Federal and national organizations and State contacts that work to prevent child abuse.

Promoting child & family well-being

Information on well-being and ways programs and systems can support it. Includes resources on protective factors, marriage, fatherhood, and parenting.

Public awareness & creating supportive communities

Tools for sharing a child abuse prevention message with your community and building community support.

Prevention programs

Standards for prevention programs, research on what works, information on the role of related professionals, and resources for specific types of programs.

Developing & sustaining prevention programs

Considerations for managing a prevention program, including community needs assessment, collaborating with community partners, family engagement and retention, cultural competence, training, and funding.

Evidence-based practice

Child abuse prevention programs and strategies supported by scientific research.

Evaluating prevention programs

Evaluating program effectiveness and conducting cost analyses. Features the Evaluation Toolkit and Logic Model Builder.

PREVENT CRUELTY TO ANIMALS

Cruelty to animals is illegal and should not be tolerated. If you suspect that someone is committing acts of cruelty toward animals, please contact your local police department or law enforcement agency immediately. For most locations in the United States, for emergency situations, you can **dial 9-1-1**.

For non-emergency situations, you can submit an online notification to the Animal Rescue Team at the Humane Society of the United States:
 https://www.humanesociety.org/forms/contact-animal-rescue-team

The following information is from the ASPCA website, https://www.aspca.org/take-action/report-animal-cruelty:

How to Report Cruelty

Try to gather the following information before submitting a report of animal cruelty:

- A concise, written, factual statement of what you observed—giving dates and approximate times whenever possible—to provide to law enforcement.

- Photographs of the location, the animals in question and the surrounding area. **Note: do not put yourself in danger!** Do not enter another person's property without permission, and exercise great caution around unfamiliar animals who may be frightened or in pain.

- If you can, provide law enforcement with the names and contact information of other people who have firsthand information about the abusive situation.

- It is possible to file an anonymous report, but please consider providing your information. The case is more likely to be pursued when there are credible witnesses willing to stand behind the report and, if necessary, testify in court.

Keep a record of exactly whom you contacted, the date of the contacts, copies of any documents you provided to law enforcement or animal control and the content and outcome of your discussion. If you do not receive a response from the officer assigned to your case within a reasonable length of time, make a polite follow-up call to inquire about the progress of the investigation.

How to Recognize Animal Cruelty

While an aggressive, timid, or fearful animal may appear to be a cruelty victim, it is not possible to know if an animal is being abused based on their behavior alone. It is best to examine the animal and his surrounding environment to determine whether or not he or she needs help.

Physical Signs of Cruelty

- Tight collar that has caused a neck wound or has become embedded in the pet's neck

- Open wounds, signs of multiple healed wounds or an ongoing injury or illness that is not being treated

- Untreated skin conditions that have caused loss of hair, scaly skin, bumps, or rashes

- Extreme thinness or emaciation—bones may be visible

- Fur infested with fleas, ticks, or other parasites

- Patches of bumpy, scaly skin rashes

- Signs of inadequate grooming, such as extreme matting of fur, overgrown nails, and dirty coat

- Weakness, limping or the inability to stand or walk normally

- Heavy discharge from eyes or nose

- An owner striking or otherwise physically abusing an animal

- Visible signs of confusion or extreme drowsiness

Environmental Signs of Cruelty

- Pets are tied up alone outside for long periods of time without adequate food or water, or with food or water that is unsanitary

- Pets are kept outside in inclement weather without access to adequate shelter

- Pets are kept in an area littered with feces, garbage, broken glass, or other objects that could harm them

- Animals are housed in kennels or cages (very often crowded in with other animals) that are too small to allow them to stand, turn around and make normal movements

To Report Cruelty Seen on the Internet

If you see cruelty depicted online, there are steps you can take to report the site or images in question:

- Access this background information for a particular website by visiting https://whois.net/ and doing a "whois" search of the site in question.

- Contact the site's ISP (Internet service provider) about the offensive material.

- If you have concrete information that a website is displaying/promoting criminal acts, you may wish to contact any or all of the following organizations and advise them of the facts of the situation:

- Local law enforcement officials ("Local" in this case means based in the area from which the website originates—the "whois" search will provide you with the registrant's address) and, if you think an animal is in immediate danger, the possible offender's local FBI branch

- Your local animal shelter or humane society, which may have the power to enforce animal cruelty laws in the area

- The local city/county Health Department/Board of Health, because abuse of animals often involves unsafe or unsanitary conditions for humans

- The Internet Crime Complaint Center (IC3), but only if what you have seen has a financial element (someone selling, trading, or offering an illegal good or service)

- Local and national media organizations, as the power of the media to bring public attention to an animal abuse situation can help initiate corrective actions

PREVENT DOMESTIC VIOLENCE

Domestic violence is illegal and should not be tolerated. If you believe that you and or others are in danger, do not hesitate and call your local law enforcement immediately. For most locations in the United States, you can **dial 9-1-1**.

The following are intended to be helpful resources:

National Domestic Violence Hotline: Our advocates are available 24/7 at 1-800-799-SAFE (7233) in more than 200 languages. All calls are free and confidential. Your safety is our priority, so all phone calls and chats are completely confidential.

Website: https://www.thehotline.org/help/

Support. Resources. Hope.

At the National Domestic Violence Hotline, our highly trained expert advocates are available 24/7 to talk confidentially with anyone in the United States who is experiencing domestic violence, seeking resources or information, or questioning unhealthy aspects of their relationship.

The Hotline provides lifesaving tools and immediate support to empower victims and survivors to find safety and live free of abuse. We also provide support to friends and family members who are concerned about a loved one. Resources and help can be found by calling 1-800-799-SAFE (7233). Individuals who are Deaf or hard of hearing may use TTY 1-800-787-3224. Additionally, advocates who are Deaf are available 24/7 through the National Deaf Hotline by video phone at 1-855-812-1001, Instant Messenger (DeafHotline) or email (https://www.thehotline.org/help/deaf-services/)

If it is not safe for you to call, or if you don't feel comfortable doing so, another option for getting direct help is to use our live chat service here on this website. You'll receive the same one-on-one, real-time, confidential support from a trained advocate as you would on the phone. Chat is available every day from 24/7/365. El chat en español está disponible de 12 p.m. a 6 p.m. Hora Central.

PREVENT HUMAN TRAFFICKING

Human Trafficking is illegal and should not be tolerated. If you believe that someone is being trafficked, please call local law enforcement, for which you can **dial 9-1-1** for most locations in the United States.

You also can report suspected human trafficking activity by calling Federal law enforcement at the **U.S. Department of Homeland Security directly at: 1-866-347-2423.**

National Human Trafficking Hotline

The National Human Trafficking Hotline is a 24/7, confidential, multilingual hotline for victims, survivors, and witnesses of human trafficking. The hotline can be reached:

- **By phone: 1-888-373-7888**

- **By text: text HELP to 233733 (BEFREE)**

- By email: help@humantraffickinghotline.org

- Online chat: https://humantraffickinghotline.org/chat

The hotline also has an online Referral Directory made up of anti-trafficking organizations and programs that offer emergency, transitional, or long-term services to victims and survivors of human trafficking.

Non-emergency Federal Assistance Telephone Numbers:

For individuals reporting trafficking activity: The U.S. Dept. of Justice Trafficking in Persons + Worker Exploitation Task Force Complaint Line: 1-888-428-7581 Open 9:00am to 5:00pm (EST)

For cases where labor exploitation is present but does not rise to the threshold of trafficking:

U.S. Department of Labor, Wage + Hour Division: (1-866-487-9243)

To report allegations of trafficking committed through fraud in DOL programs: U.S. Department of Labor OIG Hotline:1-202-693-6999 or 1-800-347-3756 and https://www.oig.dol.gov/

For information about how workers, including trafficking victims, can file a charge of employment discrimination.

Equal Employment Opportunity Commission (EEOC) 1-800-669-4000

U.S. Department of State: 20 Ways You Can Help Fight Human Trafficking in 2020

Anyone can join in the fight against human trafficking. Here are 20 ideas to consider acting on in the year 2020.

1. Learn the indicators of human trafficking on the TIP Office's website or by taking a training. Human trafficking awareness training is available for individuals, businesses, first responders, law enforcement, educators, and federal employees, among others.

2. If you are in the United States and believe someone may be a victim of human trafficking, call the 24-hour National Human Trafficking Hotline at 1-888-373-7888 or report an emergency to law enforcement by calling 911. Trafficking victims, whether or not U.S. citizens, are eligible for services and immigration assistance.

3. Be a conscientious and informed consumer. Find out more about who may have picked your tomatoes or made your clothes at ResponsibleSourcingTool.org, or check out the Department of Labor's List of Goods Produced by Child Labor or Forced Labor. Encourage companies to take steps to prevent human trafficking in their supply chains and publish the information, including supplier or factory lists, for consumer awareness.

4. Volunteer and support anti-trafficking efforts in your community.

5. Meet with and/or write to your local, state, and federal elected officials to let them know you care about combating human trafficking and ask what they are doing to address it.

6. Be well-informed. Set up a web alert to receive current human trafficking news. Also, check out CNN's Freedom Project for more stories on the different forms of human trafficking around the world.

7. Host an awareness-raising event to watch and discuss films about human trafficking. For example, learn how modern slavery exists today; watch an investigative documentary about sex trafficking; or discover how forced labor can affect global food supply chains. Alternatively, contact your local library and ask for assistance identifying an appropriate book and ask them to host the event.

8. Organize a fundraiser and donate the proceeds to an anti-trafficking organization.

9. Encourage your local schools or school district to include human trafficking in their curricula and to develop protocols for identifying and reporting a suspected case of human trafficking or responding to a potential victim.

10. Use your social media platforms to raise awareness about human trafficking, using the following hashtags: #endtrafficking, #freedomfirst.

11. Think about whether your workplace is trauma-informed and reach out to management or the Human Resources team to urge implementation of trauma-informed business practices.

12. Become a mentor to a young person or someone in need. Traffickers often target people who are going through a difficult time or who lack strong support systems. As a mentor, you can be involved in new and positive experiences in that person's life during a formative time.

13. Parents and Caregivers: Learn how human traffickers often target and recruit youth and who to turn to for help in potentially dangerous situations. Host community conversations with parent teacher associations, law enforcement, schools, and community members regarding safeguarding children in your community.

14. Youth: Learn how to recognize traffickers' recruitment tactics, how to safely navigate out of a suspicious or uncomfortable situation, and how to reach out for help at any time.

15. Faith-Based Communities: Host awareness events and community forums with anti-trafficking leaders or collectively support a local victim service provider.

16. Businesses: Provide jobs, internships, skills training, and other opportunities to trafficking survivors. Take steps to investigate and prevent trafficking in your supply chains by consulting the Responsible Sourcing Tool and Comply

Chain to develop effective management systems to detect, prevent, and combat human trafficking.

17. College Students: Take action on your campus. Join or establish a university club to raise awareness about human trafficking and initiate action throughout your local community. Consider doing one of your research papers on a topic concerning human trafficking. Request that human trafficking be included in university curricula.

18. Health Care Providers: Learn how to identify the indicators of human trafficking and assist victims. With assistance from local anti-trafficking organizations, extend low-cost or free services to human trafficking victims. Resources from the Department of Health and Human Services can be found on their website.

19. Journalists: The media plays an enormous role in shaping perceptions and guiding the public conversation about human trafficking. Seek out some media best practices on how to effectively and responsibly report stories on human trafficking.

20. Attorneys: Offer human trafficking victims legal services, including support for those seeking benefits or special immigration status. Resources are available for attorneys representing victims of human trafficking.

PREVENT SUBSTANCE ABUSE

The Substance Abuse and Mental Health Services Administration (SAMHSA) maintains a Website (https://findtreatment.gov) that shows the location of residential, outpatient, and hospital inpatient treatment programs for drug addiction and alcoholism throughout the country. This information is also accessible by calling **1-800-662-HELP.**

NIH National Institute on Drug Abuse: https://www.drugabuse.gov/publications/principles-drug-addiction-treatment-research-based-guide-third-edition/frequently-asked-questions/where-can-family-members-go-information

The **American Academy of Addiction Psychiatry** and the **American Academy of Child and Adolescent Psychiatry** each have physician locator tools posted on their Web sites at aaap.org and aacap.org, respectively.

The **Partnership at Drugfree.org** (drugfree.org) is an organization that provides information and resources on teen drug use and addiction for parents, to help them prevent and intervene in their children's drug use or find treatment for a child who needs it. They offer a toll-free helpline for parents (**1-855-378-4373**).

The **American Society of Addiction Medicine** (asam.org) is a society of physicians aimed at increasing access to addiction treatment. Their Web site has a nationwide directory of addiction medicine professionals.

NIDA's National Drug Abuse Treatment Clinical Trials Network (drugabuse.gov/about-nida/organization/cctn/ctn) provides information for those interested in participating in a clinical trial testing a promising substance abuse intervention; or visit clinicaltrials.gov.

The **National Institute on Alcohol Abuse and Alcoholism** (niaaa.nih.gov) provides information on alcohol, alcohol use, and treatment of alcohol-related problems (https://www.niaaa.nih.gov/publications/brochures-and-fact-sheets/treatment-alcohol-problems-finding-and-getting-help).

NIDA's DrugPubs Research Dissemination Center (drugpubs.drugabuse.gov) provides booklets, pamphlets, fact sheets, and other informational resources on drugs, drug abuse, and treatment.

PREVENT SUICIDE

Do not hesitate to call the National Suicide Prevention Lifeline: 800-273-8255, Website: https://suicidepreventionlifeline.org/ The National Suicide Prevention Lifeline is a national network of local crisis centers that provides free and confidential emotional support to people in suicidal crisis or emotional distress 24 hours a day, 7 days a week. We're committed to improving crisis services and advancing suicide prevention by empowering individuals, advancing professional best practices, and building awareness.

The National Suicide Prevention Lifeline is a leader in suicide prevention and mental health crisis care. Since its inception, the Lifeline has engaged in a variety of initiatives to improve crisis services and advance suicide prevention for all, including innovative public messaging, best practices in mental health, and groundbreaking partnerships.

The U.S. Substance Abuse and Mental Health Services Administration (SAMHSA) and Vibrant Emotional Health launched the Lifeline on January 1, 2005. Vibrant Emotional Health, the administrator of the grant, works with its partners, the National Association of State Mental Health Program Directors (NASMHPD), National Council for Behavioral Health, and others, to manage the project, along with Living Works, Inc., an internationally respected organization specializing in suicide intervention skills training.

The National Suicide Prevention Lifeline is independently evaluated by a federally funded investigation team from Columbia University's Research Foundation for Mental Hygiene. The Lifeline receives ongoing consultation and guidance from national suicide prevention experts, consumer advocates, and other stakeholders through the Lifeline's Steering Committee, Consumer/Survivor Committee, and Standards, Training and Practices Committee.

SEEK MENTAL HEALTHCARE

The following is from:
https://www.nimh.nih.gov/health/find-help/index.shtml:

Get Immediate Help in a Crisis

Call 911 or another local emergency telephone number (if you do not have 911 service in your area) if you or someone you know is in immediate danger or go to the nearest emergency room.

National Suicide Prevention Lifeline
Call 1-800-273-TALK (8255); En Español 1-888-628-9454
The Lifeline is a free, confidential crisis hotline that is available to everyone 24 hours a day, seven days a week. The Lifeline connects callers to the nearest crisis center in the Lifeline national network. These centers provide crisis counseling and mental health referrals. People who are deaf, hard of hearing, or have hearing loss can contact the Lifeline via TTY at 1-800-799-4889.

Crisis Text Line
Text "HELLO" to 741741
The Crisis Text hotline is available 24 hours a day, seven days a week throughout the U.S. The Crisis Text Line serves anyone, in any type of crisis, connecting them with a crisis counselor who can provide support and information.

Veterans Crisis Line

Call 1-800-273-TALK (8255) and press 1 or text to 838255

The Veterans Crisis Line is a free, confidential resource that connects veterans 24 hours a day, seven days a week with a trained responder. The service is available to all veterans, even if they are not registered with the VA or enrolled in VA healthcare. People who are deaf, hard of hearing, or have hearing loss can call 1-800-799-4889.

Disaster Distress Helpline

Call 1-800-985-5990 or text "TalkWithUs" to 66746

The disaster distress helpline provides immediate crisis counseling for people who are experiencing emotional distress related to any natural or human-caused disaster. The helpline is free, multilingual, confidential, and available 24 hours a day, seven days a week.

Find a Health Care Provider or Treatment

Treatment for mental illnesses usually consists
of therapy, medication, or a combination of the two. Treatment can be given in person or through a phone or computer (telehealth). It can sometimes be difficult to know where to start when looking for mental health care, but there are many ways to find a provider who will meet your needs.

Primary Care Provider

Your primary care practitioner can be an important resource, providing initial mental health screenings and referrals to mental health specialists. If you have an appointment with your primary care provider, consider bringing up your mental health concerns and asking for help.

Federal Resources:

Some federal agencies offer resources for identifying health care providers and help in finding low-cost health services. These include:

- Substance Abuse and Mental Health Services Administration (SAMHSA): For general information on mental health and to locate treatment services in your area, **call the SAMHSA Treatment Referral Helpline at 1-800-662-HELP (4357).** SAMHSA also has a Behavioral Health Treatment Locator on its website that can be searched by location.

- Health Resources and Services Administration (HRSA): HRSA works to improve access to health care. The HRSA website has information on finding affordable healthcare, including health centers that offer care on a sliding fee scale.

- Centers for Medicare & Medicaid Services (CMS): CMS has information on its website about benefits and eligibility for mental health programs and how to enroll.

- The National Library of Medicine (NLM) MedlinePlus: NLM's website has directories and lists of organizations that can help in identifying a health practitioner.

- Mental Health and Addiction Insurance Help: This website from the U.S. Department of Health and Human Services offers resources to help answer questions about insurance coverage for mental health care.

National Agencies and Advocacy and Professional Organizations: Advocacy and professional organizations can be a good source of information when looking for a mental health provider. They often have information on finding a mental health professional on their website, and some have practitioner locators on their websites. Examples include but are not limited to:

- Anxiety and Depression Association of America
- Depression and Bipolar Support Alliance
- Mental Health America
- National Alliance on Mental Illness

State and County Agencies: The website of your state or county government may have information about health services in your area. You may be able to find this information by visiting their websites and searching for the health services department.

Insurance Companies: If you have health insurance, a representative of your insurance company will know which local providers are covered by your insurance plan. The websites of many health insurance companies have searchable databases that allow you to find a participating practitioner in your area.

University, College, or Medical Schools: Your local college, university, or medical school may offer treatment options. To find these, try searching on the website of local university health centers for their psychiatry, psychology, counseling, or social work departments.

Help for Service Members and Their Families: Current and former service members may face different mental health issues than the general public. For resources for both service members and veterans, please visit the MentalHealth.gov page Help for Service Members and Their Families page or the U.S. Department of Veteran Affairs' mental health page.

Deciding if a Provider is Right for You

Once you find a potential provider it can be helpful to prepare a list of questions to help you decide if they are a good fit for you. Examples of questions you might want to ask a potential provider include:

- What experience do you have treating someone with my issue?
- How do you usually treat someone with my issue?
- How long do you expect treatment to last?
- Do you accept my insurance?
- What are your fees?

For tips regarding talking with your healthcare provider, refer to:

NIMH Taking Control of Your Mental Health: Tips for Talking with Your Health Care Provider fact sheet

Treatment works best when you have a good relationship with your mental health provider. If you are not comfortable or are feeling like the treatment is not helping, talk with your provider, or consider finding a different provider or another type of treatment. If you are a child or adolescent, consider speaking with your doctor or another trusted adult. **Do not stop current treatment without talking to your doctor.**